FRONT COVER:
"Our Ultimate Destination"

Man and woman, gloriously alive and glowing within, clasp hands and face the universe and the future. They are suspended above their previous existence – their auras blend in a rainbow fountain above them.

Our DNA/RNA "double helix genetic code," discovered in the 1950s, is already changing! Under the energy influences, rhythms and cycles showering the earth today, we "come alive" as we are transformed on the journey to regain our original 12 DNA strands.

BLACK & WHITE PHOTO (frontispiece):
"Humanity Today"

Man and woman stepping off the cosmic diving board together at the eleventh hour – making a 'quantum leap.' Their faith and new knowledge now take them beyond the constraints of linear time and its limitations.

Illustrations are by the noted
artist, Arthur Douët.
Contact him at:
1601 Gabriel View
Georgetown, TX 78628

(512) 863-9263

New Cells, New Bodies, NEW LIFE!

You're Becoming a
Fountain of Youth!

Virginia Essene, ed.

S.E.E. Publishing Company, Santa Clara, California, USA

Cover Art: Arthur Douët

ISBN # 0-937147-06-0
Library of Congress Catalog Card Number: 91-062236

Spiritual Education Endeavors
Publishing Company
1556 Halford Avenue, #288
Santa Clara, CA 95051
USA

First Printing September 1991
Second Printing October 1992
Third Printing December 1993

DEDICATION

Genuine thanks and appreciation to all the Masters of Love and our various cosmic helpers wherever they are in the vast, many-splendored dimensions of Light and Life.

A special gratitude, also, to all of us cosmic wonder kids on this planet whatever age we may be – young or well-vintaged. May our combined vision, our spiritual commitment and creative talents, usher in an age of cosmic wisdom and love.

And finally, special gratitude to those wonderful souls in their new baby bodies and those in their childhood years; we salute you as divine treasures! We've been waiting for you "super tots" to bring life's next evolutionary wave of superconscious humanity. With open arms and hearts, we honor and welcome you. May our experience together bring earth to heaven...and heaven to earth.

ACKNOWLEDGMENTS

I am deeply grateful to my spiritual brother, Urs Winzenried of Bern, Switzerland, for his soul commitment to the Light and his key financial support of my own spiritual writings. Without his assistance in having _Descent of the Dove_ translated into German, its recent publication by a German publisher would not have happened.

Margaretha Winzenried is also warmly thanked for her support to this current book.

Dorothy and Marcus Hermans are most genuinely appreciated for their financial and spiritual support of many SHARE Foundation efforts and projects, including this one.

Other appreciated supporters of this book's publication who deserve acknowledgment are: Shirley Grant, Bruce Lavan, Pucci, Walter Schley, Alvin Schultz, Barbara Sparks, Donald A. Stevens, Dorothy A. Turkowski and Doris M. Vaughn.

Personal thanks for their part in the preparation of this manuscript go to ♥♥♥♥♥♥♥♥♥ DaVid Barker, Diana Dunkleman, Donna Hunt, Helen Kelly, Sally Nash, Jan Ricksecker and Jim Wortman.

Finally, I want to thank all of the metaphysical writers, speakers, teachers, healers, artists, musicians, scientists, statesmen and helpers – visible and invisible – who have brought their own wisdom and love to our planet. The gifts of these masters of love have enriched my life and helped me to constantly broaden my comprehension of the cosmic nature of existence.

FOREWORD

Regrettably, space does not permit each channel to write an individual foreword, but one thing we certainly have in common is our willingness to share information. Since I am the contact who coordinated this cooperative venture, I would like to share something about my own personal journey, for I believe we all are creating extraordinary circumstances by our willingness to take positive actions, just one step at a time.

In the 1970s, when I first began to meditate, I had no idea where future events were leading, which is probably just as well. It would have been too unbelievable, fantastic and frightening. Yet I remained willing to be involved in a continuum of volunteer activities, such as grief and bereavement and hospice work, that brought me ever onward to goals only my soul understood.

During a two-year period, I experienced the deaths of the three major relationships in my life, which led me to question the meaning of life and death. As a part of my emotional healing, I became involved as a volunteer in grief and bereavement counseling.

Sitting with other human beings, listening to their pain and suffering, I began to broaden my perceptions about life, to surrender some of my judgmental attitudes, and to desire a different life for myself and everyone else on earth.

I underwent an intense spiritual questioning, which led me to search out metaphysical materials and the answers they provided. The comfort and clarity which I received from this exploration gave me a deep realization that I had to get healed so I could assist others to go within themselves to begin their own healing process.

After some years in grief and bereavement counseling, I

became more involved with people who were actually dying and needed physical as well as emotional support. So, I co-founded an eight bed hospice unit within a skilled nursing facility.

Throughout this period I belonged to metaphysical churches, joined organizations such as A.R.E., and listened to some of the early channelers like Kevin Ryerson. Then I taught a class on Comparative Religions and completed reading a set of books entitled A Course in Miracles.

At this time, I also assisted a woman called Robin Cameron, now deceased, to bring forth messages from two invisible energies: one called " The Old One," and another, "Sin-Ji." These were my first two spiritual guides. They opened my awareness that consciousness exists everywhere and can communicate even though no physical body is present.

While this was a turning point in my own consciousness, I never expected to become a channel myself, strange as that seems to me now.

Perhaps part of my resistance to channeling was due to the fear that I would lose my job as a teacher; however, a major part was due to the rigid beliefs in my own personality, and my unwillingness to change.

Eventually, though, I turned my life over to broader direction and surrendered to the request that I become a scribe for inspirational information.

To complete the first book, New Teachings for an Awakening Humanity, I took some unpaid leave from my college employment and made a time commitment of nearly a year to get the book ready for publication.

I truly expected that was the end of it, but because the Gold Ray energy of Christ Jesus wished the book to be available by Easter of 1986, I had to publish it myself.

Shortly thereafter, I was asked to scribe another book from other spiritual energies, so I took very early retirement and finished the second book entitled Secret Truths for Teens and Twenties.

I then collaborated with a spiritual sister, Ann Valentin, to bring forth a book called Cosmic Revelation. The two of us traveled together, as speakers, to many national and international destinations.

This was followed by another collaborative effort with Ann in <u>Descent of the Dove</u>, which for me finalized a series of four books originating from a variety of cosmic beings. Each of the four books differed in phases of information and energy vibration levels.

Now, a still greater task has been presented to 11 other very different channels and myself: to address the same DNA health/transformation topic, each in our own way - knowing there will be differences in explanations, ideas and suggestions.

This willingness to participate, however, even as a loosely organized group consciousness is a kind of hallmark, or step forward, in the spiritual cooperation model.

So, from our individual willingness to work by ourselves or with one other partner, we now move to working with a group of 12, that mystical symbol so necessary in our current transitional experience.

Hopefully, our goal of describing what humanity's present genetic transformation is all about, and how best to cope with its many ramifications will be only a beginning or extension of something valuable and exciting.

Humanity is in the throes of startling experiences and incomprehensible events yet to unfold.

By our human willingness as people who are reaching for group cooperation, I believe we stand on a high plateau of potentiality with enormous opportunity for growth, joy and transformation.

As we continue to be willing to experience whatever the next phase may be, miracles will occur. I believe this because I've experienced them. Even when I have a temporary detour into unlovingness, the ultimate path is so clear that I can return "on course."

What a gift to know we who choose it are all healing. And so is the planet.

Then, without knowing full details of this divine plan, let us join together in group consciousness and use our cooperative effort and energies to solve earth's problems and create the world we really desire and envision.

We twelve channels hope our model will encourage others to practice using their own group power in constructive ways.

All the participants of this book join me in wishing you well in our mutual earth adventure and inner transformation.

As shared in the book, <u>New Teachings for an Awakening Humanity</u>,

"Humanity is not alone in this Universe. Your earth is now being raised back into the higher love dimension she once held. Only those humans who choose peace will be co-creators in this cosmic process. Time is critical. YOU are needed. Will you help?"

INTRODUCTION

What is there embedded in the deep recesses of our human family's consciousness that covets better health, longer life and even immortality? Why do our world religions, myths, epics, fairy tales, sagas, and even our fantasies suggest that we are capable of being rejuvenated into good health, long life and eternal consciousness?

The belief that we humans are immortal but have somehow lost that quality whispers deep within us, and it seems natural we should balk at the condition called death. Is alchemy possible? Can we change illness and disease and negativity into health, joy and perennial youth? Health-filled longevity? Life everlasting?

Are these the dreams – even the madness – of humanity? Or is this deeply planted concept an archetype, a prevalent shared belief, that haunts our unconscious repository of evolutionary history with lingering impressions of a past truth once enjoyed?

Are we the offspring of an awesome Creator containing the cellular credentials of a prodigal birthright? Or is eternal life only an unrequited longing for a promised land never to be achieved on earth? If immortality exists, are its roots only in the invisibility of Spirit or can its heritage be claimed by us today, in our body, even as Christ Jesus demonstrated and promised?

Were the stories, myths and legends about magical springs and living waters that granted health and youthfulness, an influence behind the military conquests of Alexander the Great's expeditions? And did Ponce De Leon's external search to find the fountain of youth in Florida reflect humanity's own inner remembrance of what once was ours?

Biblical teachings from both the Old and New Testaments also link water and Spirit – water as life and water as purification. In these and other records, water was clearly believed to do more than quench thirst and grow crops. It was mystically valued and fervently honored. But why?

Is it possible that, in some encoded but suspended animation, we have held the memory of our original genetic origin and its awesome capabilities until we could evolve back in consciousness? Is this the present momentous experience in which our own inner waters — beyond blood to the flowing electromagnetic energy of molecular life — can be reclaimed? Are we, in fact, a fountain of youth, a fountain of life's vitality in which we can achieve immortality itself?

Whether you have been drawn to these tales of long-sought fountains of youth or not, you may at some time have hoped for a reprieve from the discomfort associated with death and its frequent state of pain, suffering and physical incapacities. Whether you have thirsted for eternal life, or only sought relief from these limitations of the physical body, read on. What if, whether by forgetfulness, interference or denial, we find that each human body has actually lost its fountain of youth? Is it possible that we can now genetically reclaim a spiritual and physical transformation?

Dare we think such thoughts and desire to reclaim a lost spiritual heritage?

Dare we now institute such a collective vision to attain both individual and group enlightenment?

This book explores such issues and brings current information to earth that is called inspired, revealed or channeled. The participants of these following 12 chapters will speak about this matter in very unique ways, for they are all concerned about humanity's evolutionary shift of the genetic code, our DNA/RNA patterns, into higher vibratory frequency and consciousness levels. These authors will challenge many concepts about death as an unnatural and unnecessary condition that can be circumvented or transformed, so be forewarned!

The 12 channels included here are not afraid to bring forth these different messages in their various styles and energy vibrations because they know this will be valuable. They know the variety of information will allow you to use soul resonance and personality discernment about what you recognize as your truth at this particular moment in evolution. As you might imagine, it has not been easy to coordinate collecting materials from 12 very busy people who used <u>different</u> computers and software programs! So please forgive any crowded word spacing caused by computer program limitations.

Now I ask you to join with us in this reading adventure and see it as an opportunity for you to participate as a new breed...an advanced consciousness that can be free of judgment about who is right, best, accurate, and so on - to simply allow yourself to select what feels right in its vibration and thought. Pick from the potpourri what helps your own acceleration and 'leave the rest' for now, without pronouncing it bad or wrong. Practice what we are learning about life, which is that every one of us is different and needs to be where we are. Therefore, there **has** to be variety. This is not generally the easiest thing to do, but let's give it a serious attempt.

Some of the readers of this book will be delighted and satisfied, while others may be dismayed or perplexed. We hope you will see that your emotional responses to the information are important teaching tools for yourself. Notice them because you may find many different attitudes and feelings that are unexpected. THIS IS PART OF THE INTENDED EXPERIENCE. Just notice what emotions come up for you and deal with their very origin and nature. It is obvious we each have strong beliefs and defenses about those beliefs. And of course readers are not being required to change. However, it could be a sorting out time, if this appeals to you.

In creating this book about DNA and the genetic transformation within our physical bodies, each of our 12 participants was given the same list of 10 questions to ponder and organize into a 10-15 page chapter. Each channel was free to bring whatever message their source wished so long as it was clear and well-communicated. *None knew what the others were writing!* Thus there will be different approaches and focuses in these chapter selections. Also, chapter page lengths have differed more than expected. Some will touch upon all questions briefly, but a few have elected to address some items in greater depth.

We wish to state that nothing written by any of the channels is intended as medical diagnosis or treatment.

We invite you to try out a new experiment of reading a chapter at a time as a complete presentation, rather like a cosmic essay, and to experience its energy as well as the thoughts it contains. Pause between chapters. One – or perhaps many times – we trust these presentations will trigger, register, or call forth soul recognitions that will assist you to live a more joyful and participatory life purpose.

Again I repeat, the chapters are not identical in their information so do not expect this. They may even contain contradictions. If you wish to note these – do so. But please look for commonalities, most of all, and trust your intuitive, soul self, in determining what feels right for you. Because there are many levels and dimensions of thought and energies represented here, we expect everyone can find at least one comment or explanation of value.

May we suggest you be open-minded but not gullible. Avoid rigidity, and reach for the open sky. The vibrations of these messages are powerful indeed and we hope they serve you at your present level of understanding, whatever that is, by raising questions and introducing concepts to expand your natural love and wisdom. Please appreciate that some of us are taking a risk to share ideas we believe will benefit the planet, humanity, and all of life.

We are also including a page of information about each participant's work so that you may remain in contact with those people whose messages touch you. This is another aspect of the book – to show our readers the breadth of information that exists around the country.

Finally – thank you, from all of us, for your willingness to participate with the Divine plan now bringing us back to higher consciousness...and for being our spiritual brothers and sisters in this extraordinary time of genetic transformation at many levels.

Joy, peace and light from all of us to all of you!

Virginia Essene

Contents

(continued)

Chapter 1

Christ Jesus

Channeled by Virginia Essene

I am here to inform you of crucial celestial occurrences, to explain the inner astronomy of your present life transformation, and to shepherd all who will listen through an awesome and dramatic decade of humanity's evolutionary advancement to higher consciousness. As your teacher and brother, then, I request you honor your own spiritual nature and my concern for you by listening to this present-day message, spoken in everyday language. You have enormous creative powers, mental prowess and emotional nurturance. Please apply these as you read my message, and take its meaning to your own highest consciousness for future application.

Although you are a dense physical body, you have genetic patterns within your body which are of a celestial nature. You are composed of things that the naked eye cannot see – atoms, molecules, chromosomes and cells – and their wondrous interrelationships are your physical life foundations.

Your primitive scientific instruments only now reveal the inner worlds of mysterious life plasma and divine implantations which define you and grant an evolutionary majesty you scarcely comprehend. Words like "atoms," "chromosomes," and "cells" can hardly describe divinity's creative activities, but they are at least a beginning.

Your cells contain the DNA/RNA memory codes and intelligence factors to access and fulfill their evolutionary advancement. You are a cosmic pattern or template of celestial potential. You are a sacred reflection of a new human species. You are the presence of wisdom and of love upon a beautiful planet that also has life cells and spiritual qualities.

Kindly remember both she and you are partners in this cosmic awakening experience, and treat her accordingly.

The high vibratory frequency that we are sending to assist you and the planet in this tremendous energy shift to greater consciousness has a vast invisible impact on you. Most of you are struggling to understand the full ramifications of what this means, to make sense of what you are experiencing.

In brief, you are in a **holy coordinate point**, moving beyond linear time. Physical structures are changing. This is affecting your entire beingness, including the physical body's characteristics as influenced by the soul's flowering. Because you are evolving – physically, emotionally, mentally and spiritually – you are likely to experience unusual behaviors, which are uncharacteristic of you.

It is vital for you to understand what is happening to you; therefore, many messages giving nurturance and guidance will come from many realms. I am not suggesting that anything devastating will happen to you, but some of you are experiencing unsettling phenomena that I wish to explain.

With this powerful energy shift occurring, you could notice some of the following: *heavy or chaotic emotional feelings...mood extremes...worry...an acceleration of time...lack of self-worth...self-doubt...confusion...fear.*

You may feel discouraged when trying to get things done efficiently and quickly, creating frustration and anger. You may experience short-term memory loss about names or events, or even an inability to concentrate. Material possessions may become less important to you, for these energies may demand that you examine everything in your life. The kind of work you do, the relationships you have, and where you want to live will be open to soul scrutiny more potently. You may even want to leave your present job or home and strike out for a different location and/or different circumstances to honor your soul purposes.

There may be changes in sleep patterns and food preferences. You may experience unexplainable restlessness, clumsiness or small accidents, unusual tiredness, fatigue or weariness; even minor sickness or disease. Many of you complain of some vague experiences you call "feeling peculiar."

2

Any or many of these things are potential during this relinquishment of linear time to hyperspace reality so you may become a fourth dimensional being while living in a physical body on a planet which is also shifting. One of your greatest challenges is to let go of the fear caused by wanting to control earthly circumstances which are presently under divine transformation. A lack of structure is not easy to accept!

Let me assure you, however, that these incoming energies bring healing to your soul and physical genetic body patterns. Because your soul has never lived in a human body while its cells and tissues receive these higher frequencies, some of you may be experiencing temporary difficulties. Consequently, we are guiding and assisting this healing process for all who request it.

When you came from the Creator on a high frequency energy vibration, that frequency had to be reduced, or to become denser and heavier, when you birthed into flesh bodies. Now you are reversing that process. This is a simplified explanation, but you must surely recognize that you are more than the body and have the capacity to experience a higher energy vibration, as in meditation, for example. Thus, even as you are vibrating at a fairly low frequency rate in order to exist here enfleshed as you are, your body's genetic intelligence and encoded memory patterns are awakening. Now they must be healed.

For this healing to happen, the cells must receive and retain more Light and be released of many past restrictions, limitations, and imperfections caused by your present life, and "even to the fourth generation," as spoken biblically. Which is to say, the paired chromosomes of physical qualities must be cleansed at least four generations back as far as physical body conditions, emotional attitudes, and mental perceptions are concerned.

As your earth scientists discovered in the 1950s, humanity's present genetic code is a double helix. This means there are two intertwining strands, or streams, of sub-atomic, cellular, hereditary information that form the pattern of your physical existence. During this divine transformation, there will be an "energy sparking" to revive and regenerate your body's cells. This spiritual recharge of the life plasma streams stimulates expansion from density to brightness, allowing the two helix strands or streams to expand into three, for the three to become six, then nine, and eventually the mystical 12 – the state of enlightenment. The mathematical equation for enlightenment is the number 12, taken to its full exponential expansion within the cellular structures. When all these internal chemical and electro-magnetic connections happen simultaneously, a human becomes a being of Light, and is no longer just a physical body.

This is why I had 12 disciples with whom I had shared information regarding this transformation into enlightenment. The demonstration of my physical Ascension or "translation" into a glowing, spiritual body, was necessary evidence of the truth of my teachings, and provides a model for your own potential experience. Not everybody will have the same identical experience, nor will it occur at the same time: it will come in varying stages for each person.

We wish you could see the rays and waves of energy and light – the minute frequencies and emanations – that are showering down on earth to make your transformation possible. As they thrust their forward movement into your body, for instance, you receive and absorb them through your brain's receptors where vast numbers of intricate chemical and electromagnetic activities are recorded and absorbed into your cells and the very essence of your physical body.

Until your scientists have instrumentation to measure these activities and emanations, of course, you must use your faith and intuition as guideposts during this present expansion.

Even as you incorporate this evolutionary physical change from cosmic energies into your body, you are also dealing with a number of negative man-made technological frequencies that are harmful to you and the planet. So you see, your body presently has an enormous adjustment to make! These energy frequencies of alternating current, from mechanical motors and a variety of inventions used in the military, business, industry and your personal homes, are not compatible with certain human body frequencies of direct current.

Remember that TV's, computers and a host of other gadgets can have harmful effects on your health and emotional stability, depending on exposure and how you use them; we cannot overemphasize the many challenges you face in maintaining positive thinking, emotional stability and a healthy body during this extraordinary time.

That is why we implore you to use positive thoughts and affirmations, be joyful every day, and exercise patience with yourself and others for not getting everything done speedily. Easily spoken by me perhaps, but NOT so easily accomplished by you in this period of rapid time acceleration! During this time alteration with the energy and Light penetration into your multi-leveled life cells and DNA/RNA genetic patterns, you must really be gentle with yourself and others even when you feel pushed. Like a straining engine, your body vehicle is attaining high altitudes and traversing to immense heights without any conscious map! In your mind's awareness, then, you must remain attentive to the journey, take frequent rest breaks to relax and deepen your inner guidance.

Therefore, let us encourage you to start with spiritual willingness to accept this divine experience, and allow yourself to be nurtured in its security. Begin daily to use positive visualizations, meditations, and affirmations to create emotional balance. By engaging your mind in visions of peace, abundance, and joy, you allow the divine principles of harmony, cooperation, wisdom and love to vibrate within your feeling nature, creating the life you deserve - the peace you are capable of being.

Since it is at the feeling level that humanity tends to lose its grandeur, through acts of violence and hostility, please do all you can to remain calm within and know you are capable of this wonderful shift. Many of you go to counseling or attend emotional support groups in your desire to have higher self-understanding. This is excellent! We congratulate you on your willingness. By consciously identifying and releasing false beliefs and traumatized life experiences since birth, you take major steps to free yourself from emotional morass and negative compulsions. However, some are learning to use new energy devices and alternative healing modes to heal personal emotions more quickly.

Even now, more improved techniques, substances, and devices related to emotional and physical healing are coming forth. Some are based upon releasing the compacted energies from various intersections of your body's meridians, or electro-magnetic highways. I strongly urge you to acquaint yourself with these bodily acupuncture points. You are a massive complex of biochemical systems and energy currents which must be kept balanced. New inventions are forthcoming which will use the healing vibrations of sound and color to organize your energy fields (auras) in healthful resonance and disease-free life. Unimaginable gifts are forthcoming very soon. You will be amazed!

However, beloved souls, to take advantage of these extraordinary new products and devices, it is essential for you to accept the responsibility of educating yourself about the true meaning of health in everyday living. If there is anything primary to your joy and success as humans attaining life mastery, it is this issue of health responsibility. Each of you is given one body in which to live and learn. The responsibility of its care belongs to the individual within it, once baby years have been safely assisted by parental or societal protection and guidance. But let me be more specific.

A human form is a creation of energy for holding consciousness in which the physical body maintains its health unless there are disruptive influences and difficulties caused by various circumstances, including the personality within. If you create powerful negative thoughts and store negative emotions over a period of time, these will eventually disrupt the balance of health and be lodged inside the body.

You can actually feel, by pressing the skin, these compressed packets or congealed globules of densified, unmoving energy. These compacted energy deposits – bumps or lumps – will create adverse effects unless their energy circulation patterns are soon restored. Consequently, it is essential that you learn not only to prevent their creation in the first place, but also to remove the past energy blockages quickly. You can learn to help yourself and others do this, though some of you may need assistance from healers who understand something about the energy circuitry of the body and who are willing to continue learning about life energy.

Those healers who use their hands in a healing procedure or process, those who do healing massage and bodywork, can often feel and release energy blockages. There are also those who apply acupressure and acupuncture to open up these blockages in the energy flow of your meridian mapways. The difficulty has been the healer's inability to simultaneously locate the unconsciousness beliefs and emotional negativity that caused them in the first place, while simultaneously releasing body deposits and blockages.

Of course, there are biochemical problems within the body which vibrational substances like herbs, sea plant products and proper nutrition can cure. Nonetheless, a breakdown of the human energy fields will continue to debilitate the body and cause a variety of diseases and conditions, depending on the location and severity of the blockages.

The trend you are experiencing in the health field today that you term "holistic" methods or practices is not really new. This trend represents prior knowledge from earlier civilizations and various spiritual centers where profound knowledge was known, taught and practiced. Many of these methods are re-emerging from a variety of cultures and will provide the basis of much valuable information. For the healers, especially those who attempt to treat degenerative diseases, vibratory healing is paramount in the reclamation of human vitality and health.

Then I urge you not to delay in learning everything you can about the nature of the human body as a self-healing creation, wherein fields of cooperative, interpenetrating currents maintain life itself. The harmonics of color and sound, uses of metals, crystals and minerals will be mid-steps before you eventually comprehend that the direct energy healing practice called laying on of hands and faith, or spiritual, healing can be done by humans and especially designed energy machines.

Faith healing, or spiritual healing, is the greatest of all healing powers for those who can employ it as I did. However, many today are incapable of giving or receiving it. That is why the other methods have been clarified.

The reason your learning in this area is so critical today is not just for your own release. The children, still young and being born, need this information early on! They need your support to help them remember how to maintain a healthy life. There have been past cultures which were able to teach children the inner maps of their bodily functions so well that the children could self-correct any difficulties at intital onset and avoid the disease and discomfort so common today.

This is how some humans lived hundred of years. Imagine the opportunity you have for your offspring. For do you not say in the secret sweetness of your heart, that you want your child to have a better life? And wouldn't this knowledge be the basis of such a desire? In ways difficult to describe in your present perception, you could be giving them a start toward eternal life.

Now for those healers who work primarily with emotional difficulties, may I suggest that the study of energy is also much needed? For the seriousness of mental and emotional pain left to fester in the body proper **causes** many forms of disease and debilitation.

It is propitious for you emotional therapists to develop techniques in which you can help release the bodily blockages even as you release the unconscious negative messages that hold these energy compactions in place.

Through unlocking the physical body while unscrambling the negative misinformation most humans contain in their programmed unconscious self, you can also provide the power of visualization and affirmation to complete the triad of healing desperately needed by humanity.

Since many healers have specialized just in spiritual healing, positive use of mind, emotional problems or physical disease as separated aspects, an exciting time lies ahead – a moment when all can expand to include several, if not all, aspects of energy-based health.

Thus, someone who has focused on bodywork will learn to help release negative, unconscious beliefs while giving massage or using healing energy touch. In the same way, those who treat emotional disorders may be able to touch the body or use acupuncture and find stored energy traps that will assist the release of long-stored traumas.

For those who do not wish to expand their energy knowledge and techniques, or who feel incapable of change, we note that today there are more and more healers working together. By this approach, healing can be focused by highly directed intention for quick recovery.

You were never meant to suffer, beloveds, so let us begin humanity's educational program about energy today. Teach the marvels of the human body, teach its natural energy functions and implement its current use, even as you learn to operate an automobile.

I beseech you to stretch your willingness to learn what causes your body to function painlessly so you can enjoy life and let the heaven you deserve beam its health-granting essence into the corridors of your existence. Every living person should make the understanding of life energy a **primary** focus in education at home or in the schools – in all subjects and in all media such as TV, movies, radio and printed form. You are a sacred functional lifeform, slightly 'out of kilter' through ignorance and emotional upheaval, but we are here to help you regain joyful balance in health.

When humanity's emotional nature becomes healthier, emancipation from disease will become more common, and stress more manageable. To prevent stress and release yourself from its effects, please do those things frequently recommended: eat healthy foods...avoid toxic drugs...establish exercise periods for free-flowing bodily movements...have quiet times...commune with nature...and don't force yourself to do all the unnecessary running around engendered by materialistic societies.

Because your body's biorhythms are a reflection of the night and day hours, and are consequently changing as time shifts, sleep when you need it – not out of forced habits. Relax frequently. Use mini-breaks and short respites to accomplish tasks more easily. Reorganize time to serve, not master, you. If you find you tend to be more forgetful, write notes or make lists and be satisfied when major things are accomplished.

If your body seems clumsy, remember that it is learning how to move at a higher frequency. Love it. Thank it for becoming a heavenly vehicle. Be grateful that you can focus your energy on creating peace and preserving life on the planet, rather than just filling your hours aimlessly. And when time seems to have vanished while you were completing a task, move from anger or frustration as quickly as possible, and rejoice that the linear, third-dimensional realm is being elevated another level toward higher consciousness. This should replace any hopelessness and confusion with joyful anticipation!

Please stay connected every day to your own expanding inner kingdom and soul residence which has its spiritual goals to complete. If your body is weary or your emotions are malcontent, slow down and merge into the holiness you truly are. Be still. Be loved. When you and your fellow compatriots can each do this, and share affectionate nurturance with each other, your body cells virtually sing with healthy life. As you frequently join together for group meditations and manifesting purposes, group consciousness will expand exponentially and you will reach the shores beyond time which is heaven indeed.

Dancing, singing and joyful sharings from natural things also help to bring heaven to earth. Laugh! Laugh long and hard. The spontaneity of joy is the partner of love, and love is your true inheritance. Physical movement is greatly needed by your body's physiology, so have a change from the excessive mental activities you maintain. Go outdoors. Breathe! Move! Enjoy the body's vitality. It is a precious resource.

This is vital, because the high quality of your vibration magnetizes positive experiences to yourself and spreads the light to others. I say to you that you are expanding into Beings with the great glowing halo you have seen painted by artists of the saints and angels.

As the next months and years progress, many of you will feel somehow lighter on your feet, be sensitive to energies around your body, see colors more vibrantly, hear sound more cosmically, and sense that your contacts with other people need fewer words.

You may begin to send and receive telepathic thoughts from others, both of this earth and also from the heavens beyond. You may realize sudden plans that need to be made, have clearer dreams and expand your intuitive sense of knowing things you haven't read or discussed on this earth. And you will continue to have more and more synchronistic events and occurrences.

There will be moments of confusion, possibly, as you leave the structured realm of third-dimensional consciousness and advance to the wonderful sphere of instant manifestation in the fourth or astral dimension. At times like this, we recommend that you frequently pause, breathe, relax and still your mind.

Understand that your consciousness is phasing back and forth between two worlds – the third and fourth dimensions – which is why you may notice an acceleration in your experience of time. Doesn't it seem to evaporate? Simply vanish? Your earth life has less solidity and structure than it used to. Remember, you are becoming less earthly and more airborne. Your expanding inner light is affecting your bodily reality.

If you drive past a roadway turn and wonder why you did that, don't blame yourself for not being better organized. Relax. Unsettling things now happen more often, and you need to be soothed, not upset and nervous. It is essential to quickly transform all upsets and negative thinking.

DO NOT FOCUS ON NEGATIVITY. This is why we direct you into your spiritual friendships more and more often, and suggest you group together for frequent discussions and joyful activities. Singing, dancing, hiking, loving interaction and consensus decision-making focused on the highest and best good for all concerned are encouraged.

As you experience this shift's potency, the challenge is to maintain your balance so that group consciousness can be empowered to its next cosmic thrust of spiritual cooperation and governance not practiced on earth in thousands of years.

You are now coming to the enviable position of practicing spiritual governance, or wise decision making, at the following four levels:

- wise and loving governance in your own personal life affairs
- peaceful pairs or partnerships of two
- wisely governed groups and organizations (three or more)
- networking among the many larger groups

This spiritual decision-making, in every situation, can be done for the highest good of all concerned and can bear the energy of the wisdom and unconditional love which was previously known only to a few, like your biblical Solomon.

You will recognize that when many come together and work in unity, no one individual has to do it all. Group consciousness can create higher and more frequent levels of manifestation for personal and planetary good than separate individuals can accomplish.

As your spiritual nature expands more and more in these coming months and years, the cosmic glow of Christhood will shine in and through the very core of your body. Your hands will be able to touch the unsettled and sick of heart and mind so they can be comforted. Your soul will envision the future of a bright and golden time and join with others who know this vision as well.

Then will you use your DNA/RNA rehabilitated bodies to implement that vision? Close your eyes for a moment and just sense, feel, or know that my statements – nay, my promises – are valid. For the promise is you, and you are being raised back to the level you held before that circumstance of separation was suffered.

By your willingness to understand and cooperate, a sacred plan at this **holy coordinate point** will be manifested. No more that this willingness is requisite, yet no less will bring the accomplishment forth. Then share the plan, please, and honor those whose lives are demonstrating it here on earth. For some the process is hardly underway; for others it is nearly complete.

You are all transforming, but we perceive you are not helping your own transformation as much as you might.

Then let me be absolutely precise and practical with you, dear ones, even as we speak of these enormously vital cosmic concepts. I strongly recommend and urge you to draw up a weekly calendar with 24 hourly spaces under each day of the week. Upon it, block out your normal sleeping times, eating times, spiritual meditation or quiet times, your employment schedules, if any, and add these up to see how many hours you have counted thus far.

Many of you do this already in order to maintain your sanity in a far too busy schedule. However, I also ask you to see how many hours you spend with caring and loving people and animals. How many hours are you out gardening, walking or exercising in nature, and how often do you have experiences and activities that make your life meaningful, whether it be music, art, reading or other joys?

Then if you are not tithing yourself at least 10% of your weekly hours to a non-stressful, joyful life, I beseech you to restructure your life so you DO spend a minimum of 10% just for you, every day if possible - 10% every week without fail! That means at least 2-3 hours daily for you or 16-17 hours weekly for your spiritual, mental, emotional and physical health.

There has never been a greater time for you to be relaxed and at peace than now, and I desire that you see it not only as an investment for you personally, but also as an investment in our divine plan for this planet's evolution in which you play a valuable and worthy role with us. When you are rested and joyful, it is far easier to receive dreams, to listen within and feel our comfort and guidance as you live each day. So kindly treat yourself with respect and a health-producing regime that permits these days of cellular transformation to transpire pleasantly as we wish the shift to occur.

Your body now needs more care than ever before and we want you to know we expect you to tithe this time of rest, reflection and joyful life participation without one trace of guilt or self-blame. If you are free to do more than this, or need more than the 10% personal time, we trust you to balance your life so there is opportunity for self-growth and service to the planet and all of life.

Please consider these words carefully and value yourselves as we acknowledge your importance in this extraordinary time of awakening.

Your many guides, teachers and I have been attempting to suggest these things to you in the quiet of your meditations. Now I have also spoken it aloud to your everyday consciousness in this very genuine appeal to joyful sanity and physical health. If our eyes could meet, I would smile my encouragement, and if our arms could entwine I would fill you with the light of understanding this request expresses. I would fill your soul with the peaceful certainty that you are truly valued. Perhaps you might take a moment to close your eyes this instant and imagine such a meeting between us, for I respect you greatly and love you eternally.

I am not dead or far away in some past historical event. I am with you now as all of us are with you if you choose it! It is no exaggeration to state that this connection is more precious than money and jewels. A day will come again when you truly experience the truth of these words.

When group consciousness is achieved the true meaning of peace will be understood and practiced, and at last a multi-dimensional reality will be yours once more.

I hope I have explained the more personal aspects of this DNA/RNA transformational shift sufficiently. Now, for those who are interested, I would like to give some additional information about this **holy coordinate point** you are in.

Please recognize that, far beyond humanity's present understanding, there are vibratory influences, purposes, and energy configurations that affect an immense creation and a life plan broader than that controlling your small planet, your solar system, or even your galaxy.

I speak here of the physical configurations of the universe itself. All consciousness and life stem from the original source. If these vibratory rays of Gold and Silver and various other colors, waves of light, rhythms and cycles did not exist there would be no orderliness and assurance of constant potential to initiate new, and support established, divine creations in their awesome variety.

Therefore, it is necessary to understand these energy rays, beams, rhythms, streams and cycles, for they presently bring immense power in their unseen vibrations and God-intended multi-dimensional purposes.

All consciousness and life stem from the original Source and its two aspects we call the Gold and Silver Rays which are from regions unspeakably distant yet intimately present. They are the matrix of all that is needed to create all physical planetary structures and living souls.

At the initial creation of material world life, there was manifested a gridwork of these vibratory energies. This gridwork was the womb which patterned the intention of your universe and placed certain principles into effect that contained an evolutionary plan.

Call it the Father principle as spoken of biblically, but know that it was **both** Mother and Father and **is** the guiding force of life! Certain laws and principles exist, control and support cosmic existence, and there is a plan for both the evolution of the PHYSICAL PLACES such as planets, stars, etc., and for MAN. The evolutionary plan for MAN (male/

female) is for MAN individually and also for MAN collectively.

When MAN (a God design with many physical forms, not just your own model or type) was given free will, s/he was given the power and ability to create many things via thoughts and intentions. This is possible, of course, because the power and intention placed in the cosmic energy womb of evolution have within them the characteristics that allow things to move, to rectify, to change. Therefore every decision made individually and collectively must have an effect of some kind. This is often called cause (intention) and effect (result), about which you are already familiar.

Each of your orbital spheres, such as planet earth, also has a specific energy. Each contains a specific purpose of intention, just as you are a separate human but belong to a human family. Each of these spheres is separate, but plays a part in a solar group intention and expression.

Simply put, these cosmic energy fields and waves are the packages of power, or the force, that keep the universe going! In your dimension, just know these influences are occurring at certain time intervals. Some are short and some much longer.

My own influence has been a 2,000 year cycle called the Piscean Age, during which I have asked you to open your heart to love and forgiveness. The conclusion of my own time cycle coincides with a number of other, longer time cycles whose purpose was set by cosmic design. These time cycles keep life evolving and changing by instigating movement.

In your particular solar system, the furthest planets of your family companions in evolution are closer to earth now than they have been in 5,000 years. It is their closer physical position, influenced from even greater cycles beyond themselves in the galaxy – some nearly 30,000 years long – that infuses the planet with a variety of massive energies.

This combination of many influences intersecting on earth at the same time is what I am calling the **holy coordinate point.** This universal energy presently affects many things as it touches each of you and calls your pre-encoded cells to change. Since each of you is composed of Light with a unique energy structure, or pattern of vibrations, the implosion of the many external planetary, solar and other cosmic vibrations will affect you in different ways.

As a human being your willingness to continue learning, growing and COOPERATING with the divine plan of evolution is your spiritual signature or soul print and is recognized by us quite uniquely. Without these external spiritual vibrations; rays, beams, cycles and energies in their various rhythms, your energy would decline and stagnate. It would not shift with the spiritual opportunities to accelerate individual and group consciousness...and the healing of your living planet. The human family is now experiencing a great command to change!

When your sensory capacity expands so that you can see the Creator's sparkling essence – its vibrations, waves and fields of glowing energy – you will be thrilled. Then you will be certain how the grandeur of the Creator's womb has been utilized in all types of celestial creations and rainbow magnificence.

Indeed, beloved souls, you would be awestruck by the many projected universal applications of life beyond your planet in the vast cosmic homeland of multi-dimensional activity! Words cannot do this breathtaking panorama of creative glory true honor, but they may perhaps enliven your soul's vibration to cosmic joy, and speed you to the majesty of cosmic participation while residing in a physical body.

Just as each of you is being activated in conscious awareness by this inner vibratory initiation towards personal grace, salvation and enlightenment, so the human family is spurred towards its own group initiation by these evolutionary influences. Because these simultaneous influences come to earth and its life at this **holy coordinate point,** cosmic energies and human consciousness are in synergistic relationship.

Consciousness now has only two choices: to join in with the flow or to resist the flow. Joining can bring unbelievable miracles. Resisting it will bring the opposite. Your personal and group metamorphosis in this time of powerful cosmic alignment was foretold long ago, and now requires a balanced participation of spiritual, mental, emotional and physical expression.

You are a small vortex of connection in that plan's vibration for wise perception and loving action to be implemented. Through you, the black negativity of earth's greater vortex points can be healed by humanity's positive group intention for peace and the preservation of life.

You may call this social revolution if you wish, but it is a spiritual reformation in which freedom and cooperation among the nations sounds a clarion chord. It is a heralded time of group consciousness and spiritual governance, during which violence and ignorance must be released within each of you and within the governments, so a positive planetary solidarity can be reached.

There will be economic collapses caused by excessive material pleasure, misuse of planetary resources, and authoritarian misuse of military power for control over others by war and violence. There are as yet no perfect humans or nations, yet the divine plan inexorably moves everything closer toward that goal of vital sacredness that cannot be ignored or avoided – only prolonged.

Our plan will plumb the depths of every resistance and triumph! You will be its beloved souls, heroes/heroines and benefactors, depending on your free will choices. My beloved family of man, the road to Christendom, or Christhood while in a body, is coming nearer and nearer. The often quoted 144,000 are not only separate people, but also the mathematical formula encoded within you for your own inner enlightenment.

Many of you will be Light some years hence! Others may be enlightened even sooner than that! We are helping you reform your lost DNA codes so you will not be separated from us anymore. Thus have all your past spiritual teachers guided you through the mire of ignorance, resistance, and hatred to this shining New, Bright Star of Bethlehem - this decade's **holy coordinate point.**

They all taught you that free will responses of a positive outgoing pattern represent the way by which you can free yourself of darkness. Then commit yourself to proper use of this time shift plan. Increase your own cluster of energy and light and you will be aided to spiritual group participation and planetary success. This accomplishment is God's intention for you!

This is our pledge, also. Take this DNA reclamation and restoration program seriously, then, for it is humanity's answer to prayer. It is the ultimate grace. There is a greater divine embrace that awaits you all, my beloveds, and many like myself extend our arms to you as your spiritual ship comes to home berth. Be comforted and comfort one another. **True life is just beginning.**

Remember, I never leave you and am here to help you successfully express the magnitude of this momentous event in your life. Then rest, rejuvenate, heal and fill your being with joy and ecstasy. You come into a long-promised event – the New Bright Star of Bethlehem's appearance – destined to change the course of this planet's history through your own willingness and talents.

This decade is our appointed hour, in conjunction with the many cosmic cycles which your soul has been awaiting. Now at last, your soul – that spark of eternal spring – dances as a sunbeam lifted high in song, and wings blissfully into celestial mansions. No less vital, however, is your physical body's crowning with a fountain of rainbow sparkling energy, the genuine fountain of youth! Your dream of becoming an embodied fountain of youth is once again within human reach. Then rejoice that your transformation into the "coat of many colors" is possible and that your body's rainbow-energy will soon arch in an upward flow of eternal life, toward the heart of its Creator.

You are souls of an expanding tomorrow, seeds of a glorious creation whose origin was birthed in the stars and whose planetary destiny lies in matter and in the expansion of worlds unseen. Your cosmic heritage is being restored. It was for this I came nearly 2,000 years ago.

Yes, it was for you I came! And it is for this you, too, have come now at this **holy coordinate point** to expand beyond time into your own ascension.

See page 207 for the 1994 Update by Christ Jesus on "YOUR PHYSICAL IMMORTALITY".

Chapter 2

Archangel Michael

Channeled by
Orpheus Phylos

I come forth and bid thee, beloved souls, what is termed a greeting, with my transmutable blue flame from the auric field of the Central Sun. May the electric blue radiations safely assist in awakening you to remembrance of the higher heavens, and many worlds beyond, where I be. And also to provide a vibrational quickening of your bodies back into the stratasdome of the astral domains and etheric worlds.

My fire is one of the four elements that are the coordinates of portals to the rhythms and cycles of momentous knowledge that can open your access to the great gateways of ascension. Through the divine master plan, the Elohim, Yahweh and the Lords of Light are uplifting the lower heavens so you may pass through the corridors of high vibration once again. You are being stimulated and empowered to leave the structural world of linear time for the electromagnetic illumination of enlightenment in starlight levels where you have desired to be.

I am bringing forth now what is termed knowledge within the words of your alphabetical letters, because in the letters is the communication link to color, light and sound. Every letter has angles, and the angles cause a vibratory hook of the universal magnetic fields of great knowledge. Within the word "knowledge" there is the word "know" but also "no" and "ledge," or "no ledge," meaning no limit or unlimited.

"No ledge" takes all things out of linear understanding and automatically begins to raise it into the non-limited etheric. This level of unlimitedness was the nature of all souls who chose to come to earth long ago to this great school. How that original unlimitedness was created is way, way beyond man's comprehension, but I will say you are presently defined by a double helix genetic code whereas you formerly had 12 genetic strands, capabilities, or full knowledge. Happily humanity is moving upwards to a triple helix and eventually back to the complete 12 representing full enlightenment. (There is also the quadruple helix, in addition to those of the mystical trinities of 3, 6, 9 and 12.)

This number "12" came from the Source at the very beginning of creation. This great Source created and birthed from itself the mother part, and then expanded that monad into the duad of Father/Mother, feminine/masculine. From its masculine and its feminine, it also created the triad – its own trinity – and from that trinity came the four, or the tetrad. Thus, your earth is in the geometric symbol called the square, or the four. Four is a numerical energy that means foundation or the spiritual dominion wherein you are allowed to see where you are evolving and can release illusion. But let me say more about the number 12, which appears in so many of the world's teachings and writings.

It holds hidden universal meaning, both for you today and for the spiritual initiates of long ago. They knew secret energies and powers you have forgotten, and wanted to pass that information down to those of the pure of heart. How to do this while living in a negative, or ignorant civilization was not easy, so they would have to imbed the information somewhere the sacred-hearted ones would find and understand it.

For instance, beloved souls, if you knew a grand secret or spiritual treasure that you wished to pass along to other pure souls, where would you put it? Your past historical times have shown that murder, imprisonment, and censorship were common tools to silence the wise ones of Light. Perhaps you, like those of bygone days, would select holy scriptures or spiritual sources to house the knowledge needed to be kept alive in human consciousness. And then house its meaning on several levels – the hidden and the ordinary.

For instance, let us refer to that document you call the Bible. Now the Bible has many different idioms, levels of meaning, and later, distortions of translation. The ordinary reader may not realize it, but originally the Bible contained about 70 per cent mystical content and historical data, and was seeded with the numeric language of wise, long-ago scientists.

The number 144,000 mentioned in the Bible seems straight-forward enough, yet it has different meanings, depending upon the knowledge one brings to it. Strictly speaking, the 144,000 may appear to refer to a particular group of people. However, it also expresses other concepts.

Within the number 144,000, the separate numerals can be added up, that is, $1 + 4 + 4 + 0 + 0 + 0$, to equal the high triad of 9. This 9 is simply a representation of the Universal Love Vibration. When a being incarnates with the energy vibration of 9, it is done with the intention of raising the planetary vibration to a state of love. Therefore, the number 144,000 represents a purpose of high positive intention, not only specific head count.

Another symbol regarding the number 144,000 relates to the intricate cross-currents of energy within the body which are learning to awaken the encoded light language in the cells. This pattern will raise the body's physical vibration and cause a physical change into a brighter light body. Molecular-cellular transformation is another way of stating it.

This is what we are calling ascension beyond personal enlightenment. Ascension can be individual or group. There is so much more to say about ideas such as these, some hidden for safekeeping in documents like the Bible, but perhaps these examples can provide a catalyst for further understanding.

Today, souls are coming to a state where the Light can bring their greatest birthing. This Light is going to show you that mankind has gone into its upward evolution. There are those who have aspired to the process of evolution. These souls can now come into their enlightened bodies. You will still maintain somewhat of a physical body, but it is going to uplift your vibratory rate so you hold a semi-physical form called physical-etheric.

All this can occur, beloved souls, because eons ago there were those created beings called Lord gods, lesser gods, angelic essences and the hosts within the hosts. There are what is called the Elohim. Elohim are the great externals and central throne counselors of the Lords of Light where many worlds were created. There is that of the great YHWH, Yahweh, the cosmic force energies of higher vibrations releasing laser light whirlwinds of advancement into your planetary system.

With aid of the Yahweh and the Elohim energy, man is able to be birthed back again into higher vibration. That means all souls who are ready are going to come back into the Law of One. What does that mean? The Law of One is All That Is in its perfection. That means, beloved souls, it is peace; it is love. It is wherein the androgynous Self can come forth and begin to reign during the Golden Era.

The important clarification needed is that eons ago there were gods who chose to come on Earth because it was assigned by great appointment. Using the very nature of Source, they created a magnificent planet called Earth, Terra, then called Shawn. There are those of the angels, also termed fallen angels, who simply chose to separate from the Source called One. From this separation, they were going to lose sight of the great Law of the Golden One, which means the perfection of themselves, and create a dual reality.

They would have to experience the scope of dual realism to its fullest by dividing into a positive and negative, or into extremes of left or right, dark or light. And then they would begin to fulfill themselves in this school.

Terra, the Earth as you know it now, is a magnificent school, a great learning place. It is held very close unto the Father's bosom. So when the fragments, formally called angels, willingly came to Earth, they knew they would have to evolve and even have to go through the "Doors of Death," for previously "the gods" did not die.

So if you think about it, it was a great sacrifice for the soul to choose to come into this experience. That separation created the laws of both darkness and the laws of Light. Yes, all souls would have to go through a time when the cell memories would not recall their perfection; therefore, each would remain for a time under the laws of karma or the laws of reincarnation. It is the process of evolution. It is how one begins to come out of the shadows of darkness into a consciousness of Light. When it is conscious, it can begin to use its universal mind and the gifts of the resurrected body. The resurrected body is what you are calling an etheric body. It is the Christ body.

Therefore, this fragment – this soul vehicle you have here on earth – is simply the fragmentization that took on the role of playing human. Through its experiences, the physical body finally regains its consciousness of Light and Light begins to feed through once again, so the vibration can be uplifted.

Presently the vibration of the universal electromagnetic fields balances this process so that the power of the ultraviolet ray, the infrared ray, the gamma ray and the source of the Central Sun are influencing evolution. This happens to you automatically and as it does, your molecular nature begins to increase in cellular vibration to a higher light quality.

When this occurs, your higher mind is going to become more predominate over the nature of the intellect, or ego, so you can learn how to use the tools and techniques of the resurrected body. You see the Christ body holds all gifts, all abilities, all power. As you begin to raise your vibrations by becoming Light or wanting to become the manifestation of that Light endeavor, the Christ energy can come through those who are ready. Then the Christ consciousness will reign on earth because these former gods will be awakened. They will utilize their gifts positively and the gifts are many! How they use their gifts in their physical activities then demonstrates who they truly are.

While you are here on earth, the most vital thing to remember is that your genetic code is energy. That genetic energy came from the original gods and also the angelic essences who came to reign over primitive man. The genetics of energy began long ago and affect you still! This started on earth with the beginning civilizations called Lemuria, Adona and Atlantis. We will speak about Lemurian energy first since these were the gods, the giants, that came to reign over man and later intermingled with the sons and the daughters of man.

The lifeform called man had already begun, meaning some fallen angels had come down on earth and were then placed into the created nature of dual reality. The word "man" means a soul who chose to come into the very nature of the principle of solidity. Here it would learn to evolve, to come into the consciousness of a higher vibration and into a godhood life. There were other gods who often chose to come to teach man and in so doing, through the weakness of desire, they also began to marry the sons and daughters of man.

This is when the genetic patterns began to separate. The first Lemurians were totally androgynous, spiritual and in the Law of One. They were without suffering from the pain of dual reality. This period was very early history before they began to war among themselves and subsequently create the thought form of negativity, which is offered to all levels of evolution.

Those who later abandoned the judicious wisdom of the Law of One wanted to take what was not theirs. They wanted to control others, to create adversity and perform destructive activities. This is when the brothers and sisters of Lemuria began to separate among themselves and cause a divided race. Atlantis and other places were later colonized by the dissidents, thereby creating two major civilizations.

Some peaceful Lemurians migrated across what you term the many continents, into Asia and Egypt. The great beings travelled extensively, even into these lands of your world today, such as the USA, because at that geological period there were no Atlantic and Pacific Oceans.

The Lemurians realized how the negative Atlantean brothers were going to cause a destruction based upon the highest technologies they could utilize - the technology of the crystallization of the power of their minds! Eventually the Atlanteans did cause a great destruction of their empire by earthquakes, even before its final sinking. Although the negative power prevailed in Atlantis, an Atlantean minority still wanted to use only constructive power. This positive minority migrated to Egypt, the Orient and India. Therefore two groups existed, those who were of the Light and those who created the total destruction of Atlantis.

How you can determine the genetic separation into those two early influences of light and dark energy intention is by noting that Adam and Eve are names used to symbolize the <u>atoms</u> and the <u>ev</u>olutionary period. There are many Adams and many Eves!! Many genetic changes!

Adam means red, the red man. The important issue is that as the red man migrated through many generations, climatic changes and different environments, other races developed from the red – the black, the yellow, the brown and the white race. This is when the genetic trail of separation accelerated.

How can you tell the Lemurian genetic code from the Atlantean even today? You can see the behavior of the red races, as in the American Indians, but also in the other four racial colors who have gone through all the genetic processes. Those who have evolved previously into positive and negative are being reactivated now.

For example, the Hopis and the Plains Indians, who are very, very peaceful, are still genetic carriers of the mind concept of the Lemurian energy. The more war-like Atlantean nature can be seen in those called Comanche or Apache. It does not mean it is right of wrong. It simply demonstrates the genetic process wherein the red man still holds the nature of those two soul patterns, even in those who choose to come back into the body now.

Today, the Atlantean energy is very predominate in technological countries, in all racial groups, and many scientists are working to clone life and to create cyclotronic weaponry. As in times gone by, many are using the computer and crystalline sophistication of technology to control man. So you can understand that the Atlantean energy continues in those beings who have chosen not to change and still favor destructive activities. The Lemurian energy souls are also coming forth to work for peace and restoration of the Law of One. There are many Atlanteans who have come back now in the Lemurian energy period seeking to redo what once was done incorrectly. Yet we observe many have forgotten a purity of motive.

I am giving you the definition of Lemuria and Atlantis

with their genetic subdivision so you can look at your whole world and see where it is more peaceful and where it is not. You can easily determine where the Lemurian energy predominates in contrast to where the powerful God energy of the Law of One was misused by the Atlanteans through violence and war. That God energy is how they created the great civilizations and then continued downward through the genetic process, through many generations. This is variously called the wheel of life, evolution or reincarnation.

The Lemurians and the Atlanteans who chose the positive Golden Ray, primarily migrated to Egypt. It was they, in the very beginning of Egypt, who were the Pharaohs, the winged Pharaohs, the priests, the priest class, the priestesses who still held the Law of One, meaning their androgynous self. (Not the Pharaohs through the dynasty group!) They had not separated into the dual reality because they had still not married with the sons and daughters of man. Consequently they still held the very high technology. They were asked by the greater gods to migrate and begin to live among and teach man.

This talk of greater and lesser gods may be difficult for your beliefs, since we know many of you on earth have thrown out the many Gods for the One Creator. We are suggesting you consider One Creator plus many created lifeforms without physically dense bodies, like yours, that differ from each other in their size and quality of energy vibration.

Do your best to accept that there are many different varieties and qualities of light beings who have been here at different times. Until you can regain clairvoyant capabilities and discern the variations of light quality in these beings, we will use god with a little "g" and hope for the best. When once again you can see different densities, colors, shapes and forms of light not embodied in matter, this will all make perfect sense!

Physical man did not know how to build things but the gods did. Man did not have that mathematical skill. Man did not have a calendar. It was these gods who settled in such areas as Peru and South America who taught the Mayan, the red man. These gods opened neophyte schools, called arcane mystery schools, and they taught humans to use these great gifts of the higher mind, or the higher Christ body, only for the benefit of man. That is why the rules were so rigid, and they had to swear a vow of secrecy.

Understand that the inner world is different than the inner earth. Inner world is another dimension. It is a far greater crystallization of light, and where these are located in your mountain zones or megalithic or monolithic structures, the beings of Light who reside there are the ones who are here in service to help evolve man.

The gods of this era knew how to go down into the inner worlds, or dimensions, of the golden pyramid, using silver light energy. Near the sphinx in Egypt, there was once a magnificent universal magnetic field, like a staircase, that could be used by those having etheric bodies. Man could not see it, but the physical-etheric gods could. They could rearrange the vibrational fields in order to open the entrance, using the harmonic sounds of their high telepathic mind. Thus they were able to interpenetrate energies and meet the ascended masters, the divine ministries, or the gods, who reigned as a part of these great worlds.

These gods of early Egypt had the ability to go through initiation from within the inverted position of the pyramid. (Not the outer position, which was used for man.) However, as the gods travelled around the earth in their teaching duties, they could foresee the future intermingling of themselves with man. This is when they put all they knew into a thought-guard, or a crystallized form of color, light and harmonic sound, which they could later retrieve. They could see into many lifetimes, when some of the gods would go forth, live among man and experience reincarnation. They knew the genetic cell memories would begin to release a little bit more with every reincarnation and one day they would evolve back into light consciousness. That is why some beings experience an incarnation with an awakened memory as a wonderful composer, a great philosopher, an inventor or a healer.

Think of all those beings over the eons of time who, in spite of rejection, have dropped spiritual seeds to help humanity evolve, thus assuring this planet's educational program. Today there are many of you awakening into your own godhood, who will create a new world by your model. You will teach others how to raise their physical body vibrational pattern to attain a physical-etheric embodiment.

Yes, everything is in a process of evolution, now, so the healers and teachers who wish to assist others must recognize that everyone is different. No one technique works for all because people's genetic coding is different. Yet those who are ready to seek their etheric, or enlightenment, body must learn four keys to utilize universal mind. Persons must know absolutely that they have personally experienced the energies of manifestation so profoundly that they can go forth and teach what has been personally learned. They are now to model their knowledge and share their experience of effective mind power.

The *four* keys to universal dynamics of mind are:

Relaxation, Concentration, Visualization and Affirmation.

Relaxation means you are learning how to open the doors to your inner world. It can be through meditation. It can be just simply sitting alone in a place that is serene. You bring the serenity and tranquility into the mind, emotions and body so you are calm. As you do this you leave what is called the physical world to find your inner world.

The busy mind can be scientifically identified as the rapid Beta level Hertz brain waves pattern. When you cease thinking consciously all the time and relax, you leave Beta and you go into a slower Alpha level. From the Alpha you can go into Theta and finally into the Delta state. As you go deeper and deeper into the Theta and the Theta-Delta, before sleep, you surrender into what is called the Law of One consciousness.

That is why those in meditation may find themselves going into the Circle or into what could be called a Vortex. They leave the physical dominion to go into their inner soul world, into their resurrected Christ body. Then they can open what is called the doorway to self-knowledge and have "No ledge," no limit. They can then release the seed allowing a gift or vision or a telepathic communication to occur. It is important to relax so each one can find the inner world.

After the inner world of relaxation is achieved, there is a *concentration* level that must be held. In the concentration level there is surrendering in total trust to entering a God-empowered reality. In that deep concentration you begin to develop and apply the *visualization* concept. Those having cancer, leukemia, AIDS, etc. must get into their inner world because it holds the etheric vibration of the Central Sun that can manifest positive change in its outer world body.

So you can take yourself down in consciousness by brain wave shifts and begin to visualize your body. You first must talk to your unconscious mind because it was created as your manifesting tool. It takes everything that you think, totally and exactly as you speak it, and processes that intention. So as you think it, it will be, which is why you must be very cautious and very careful how you think! As you come into the greater Light, that Light consciousness helps to create the positive force over the negative. But you must also learn to look at the negative force and become aware of those thoughts as they come into the body, so they can be recognized, stopped...and then processed into the higher supermind as positive.

The unconscious mind is like a doorway. It receives thoughts from the conscious mind which it immediately processes. So if you are aware that you are thinking "I can't," and you immediately notice and use the positive power of central mind from the Central Sun (the resurrected Christ body), it is immediately cancelled and shifted. There is nothing a soul cannot do, even the healing of its body self.

Thus, you must quiet the personality to allow the soul to create a positive picture to be deposited into the unconscious mind. Do this by calling to your God mind or Christ self and say, "God mind, tell my brain that I am healthy and I am happy today." You never say, "I will be." You must absolutely be in the now. Because if you think it now then it is now. It will be manifested into your linear outer world through the linear time process.

Remember, you have an inner library or akashic record depository that you can access. You can say, "I want to look at my books." Then when you look through your books, maybe the book will be old. Maybe it will be about greed. Or maybe the title of the book will indicate anger or guilt.

It can indicate those things that you need to get rid of. So you acknowledge negative aspects and tell your God mind, or your unconscious, to put it into the waste basket and throw it away. Get rid of all the negation or the negativities of thought! But this may be a long process. Sometimes when you look at your inner library, you see a beautiful book that is white with gold letters on it. Perhaps it is the book of health and happiness, or a similar positive suggestion. You affirm, "Yes, I am healthy and happy now. I am accomplishing all my desires now. I am fulfilling all my goals now. I am highly successful now." The key word is now, because remember the word know or knowledge also contains within its vibrational pattern the harmonic sound of the word now. **Affirm positive ideas every day, every hour if possible.**

That is why I tell people to avoid saying, "I believe this or that," but to say "I know it." When you know it, you *now* it. Therefore it is. The creation of super-conscious mind is magnificent.

Mind can always overcome matter. But it takes concentration. It takes visualization. It takes affirming you are a great being of Light accomplishing wise and loving life patterns. It takes time for you to enter your inner world and to trust your Source to perfect anything in the outer realm. It takes courage. It takes strength. And it takes discipline. What is discipline? Discipline, beloved souls, contains the word disciple. Is it not so that all beings or disciples are coming into the four L's of the cross? Not the cross of crucifixion but the cross of enlightenment. The equilateral cross shape is where the genetics of energy are now represented by the symbology of geometry. This cross of enlightenment has four L's.

Stop a moment, please, and draw over this equilateral cross that looks like a big plus sign.

Making a center dot, can you then trace 4 different printed capital letter L's starting from that point? The first is easily seen at the top right side. To its left can you see a backward capital L? Can you see two more capital L's on the bottom side of the cross like these two, making a total of four?

These L's stand for the major concepts you might express on earth to achieve enlightenment as Christ Jesus did. **Law... Life...Light...Love.** For in their full application you can be personally transformed. The first L is Law. Law is also called system and order. It is the Law of the Great Balance. It is the law that creates discipline because without discipline, you cannot have divine rank and order.

Through discipline, the disciples of the Christ, or Light, are awakening to the memory of Law. Law then connects into the vibration of the L called Life. That is the vibration, the vibratory level, that you are living in, that is in accordance with where you have evolved through many levels of reincarnation. It is not all the same in each soul. What is important is that all are evolving now from Life into Light, the ethereal understanding of the higher Spirit self, or the resurrected body. It is simply wherein the Creator is allowing the gifts of power, the gifts of mind, to become manifested through the physical form.

Then Light becomes Love. Light becomes the highest Self which is Love, unconditional Love. That means, beloved souls, there is no longer a journey because Light also knows darkness. It understands the validity in its separation. It understands that you must love the Law wherein darkness is as much as the Law of Light. The Law of One contains both. It simply seems to have separated itself on earth, here in this dimension. Therefore, you cannot be without darkness and you cannot be without Light. Light is with darkness, darkness is with Light to create the magnificence of what is called Oneness.

The four L's are also a representation of the four archangels and the four elements they utilize. So in the true cross, the four L's tell how this world was created. It is fire because I, Archangel Michael, bring you energy from the Central Sun. Archangel Raphael is the over-viewer of the air, the breath, the oxygen. Archangel Uriel is the water, which is also the hydrogen and carries the unconscious. Archangel Gabriel holds the law that is energy, solidity, and Archangel Gabriel is presently rearranging the carbon element to silicon, silica, crystal light energy from the dust of the earth to the geometrics of a *solar cross*. Your world is now changing its form into the geometrics of the resurrected cross and humanity knows it not.

All of these elements affect your body, especially the brain and your genetic code. Your brain is the transistor that the Creator put into this body vessel, to connect your intellect or ego with the higher embodiment of your Light body. Thus you can have what is called magnificent communication. Your brain is made of electrical current, electrical charges, positive and negative from the magnificent fire substance of the Central Sun. Your brain is made up of matter. You could call it a generator that holds the impulses of this magnificent electrical current. Your brain also has a liquid which contains hydrogen and that liquid brain process carries the electrical current impulses of the levels of unconsciousness.

Therefore, it is very necessary to obtain oxygen from your breathing, because it impulses life into the workings of the brain. The brain can carry those impulses to every body part, genetically, and through every vibration of every organ. Every organ holds a different vibration, yet within its composite it holds the total vibration of the Law of One. When the vibration becomes imbalanced, it is because you are thinking negatively. Buying into and holding on to the illusion of "I can't" causes self-harm since it is a negatively charged order that must be experienced once you have created it.

The genetic system of mind is being used negatively by humans who believe limited thoughts caused by worldly illusions they see about them. If you believe the illusions of limitation your innate inner power will create it. So I would give this major suggestion to man. Become more and more aware of your thought processes!! This is the process of the awakened for as you become aware that you have just said, "I can't," you say immediately, "I can." Then you have stopped the negative process. Every thought is like a "Y" in a road. It is a choice deciding your future destination! Choose to go into the positive current of your own higher enlightenment by neutralizing and transmuting the dark aspects of negativity. When you neutralize it, you have bettered it.

Promise yourself to be a clear and concise thinker about the quality of your own life. That concept of positive thinking has been popularized over the recent decades yet billions of people have not mastered its practice into their everyday affairs. People must intend what they want, beloved souls, and consistently practice the four rules I have given (as have many others with their own variations). Memorize and use them, please:

Relaxation   - **Be still.**

Concentration   - **Stay awake, be alert.**

Visualization   - **Picture how you want things to be.**

Affirmation   - **Insist it is happening NOW.**

Need I comment that each of you is part of a network of power for either positivity or negativity on this planet? That is why I persist in asking you to heal yourselves and attain self-maturity through utilizing the rules of positive manifestation. The spiritual desire for peace, wisdom, love and joy can be envisioned with highly concentrated power when many are in common agreement about human motives. Then what you learn personally can affect yourselves, the family, the community, the nation, the world - and far beyond.

I assure you that energy is a commodity of sorts upon which worlds and galaxies depend. Only your free will formulates how that energy is personally, socially or cosmically spent. You may see earth's results today, but you cannot perceive how you affect the solar system and beyond. Then let us agree, beloved souls, to be connected in spiritual mind-intention with a generous sprinkling of cosmic laughter. Laughter helps your cells raise their frequency and is most healthful indeed.

Positive thoughts are the most powerful medication your body can experience because they activate the two glands that control most brain/body functions - the pituitary gland and the pineal gland. These two hold all the medicine that anyone could ever have.

Before I leave you, beloved souls, I want to describe what your 21st Century may be like so you will have assurance and confidence that the next twenty years will be a powerful cleansing and healing era leading to an inordinately thrilling future.

Thus do I say that some of you will see the heavens opened and the earth's canopy filled with the brilliance of twelve great suns! Suns (sons) that are the legions of Light come to restore peace by the magnificence of cosmic harmonic chords. This celestial majesty will open the auric God-seal above your head and bring upliftment from your lowered state of consciousness and genetic definition.

You will continue in a new dimension of unspeakable love, in a light body which will not age. Then the counselors of time will meet together and ask all to participate in giving the children their rightful place in the evolutionary seeding of a new earth. Your children are here to bridge this interim period with their greater capacities in which they can utilize sophisticated higher mechanisms of cosmic energies and biochemical fields.

After a great cleansing and rearrangement of the favored few leaders, a new government under the Law of One will come forth to empower peace. Those places of spiritual joy called the tabernacles and temples of Light will be reopened instantaneously to bring cosmic healing through vibrational rejuvenation chambers of color and sound. The solidity of nature will be brought into nuclear, atomic structure and higher cosmic components so that every phase of life will be affected.

Food needs will be transformed. Water will remain but with a different atomic structure. Architecture of the whole world will be re-erected by focused crystal power of mind images and pictographs. In those times, you will travel in tube trains where your form moves by the momentum beyond the speed of light and you will be capable of teleportation beyond structured thought, as your movies now begin to demonstrate.

The tabernacles of knowledge and learning will have cone-shaped alloy helmets with crystal assistance to aid in acquiring greater mental capabilities. Scientists of purity will have equipment and knowledge of cosmological patterns and the higher mathematical skills using galactic tones.

Those in the communication profession will learn that your solar planet, Saturn, has rings that resonate great harmonic chords and specialized frequencies of great value for those in this universe. Historians will hold open the doors of sealed remembrance into long-forgotten truths. Some will act as doorkeepers to ley lines and pyramidic information whose structures dot all planetary objects throughout all dominions. Records from what you call akashic portals will be revealed but protected.

Those you call teachers and counselors will be assigned a variety of opportunities to inspire physically embodied souls needing guidance. Some will prepare those who have never been embodied as to how to enter solidity and express the Light of mind over matter. Others will guide individual souls. Many will be needed to implant seeds of soul purpose and empowerment for the newly developing planetary settlements throughout the endless creative expansion of the Creator's will.

Future birth processes may be artistic or reproductive. Etheric souls will be able to achieve mind to mind thought connection, through vibrational means, to birth a flame of fire. The flame of fire is a seed of crystal incubation which can create a birth, not of a helpless infant but of a child about twelve years old.

Creative endeavors in what you call music will use celestial tones in high frequency compositions seen, heard and felt. Artistic expressions, also, will combine new methods such as alloys for sculptured pieces utilizing precious healing stones. Color-coded paintings will advance higher dimensional images of beauty and joy rather than those lower vibratory visions of rage, pain and suffering common on earth today.

Once you have gained a cleansed mind, you will not vibrate to the misery of shattered emotions because you will be a master of your inner worlds and they will magnetize you into realms called genius.

You came to bring God into matter. Your mastery makes you eligible for knowledges beyond my telling, but be assured those in service to the Creator will be advanced to the highest level their vibration, intention and higher mind can magnetize and match. Know, beloved souls, the Light comes through thee by your free will decision and application of love and wisdom.

Gratitude and appreciation are important, beloved souls, so be grateful for the Creator...for your own light body...for the conscious awakening you are experiencing...for your wonderful planet earth with its beauty and nourishments of food – its animals, birds, plants, rocks and minerals. Be grateful for the greatest and smallest of wonders and remember to acknowledge the sweetness of touch, a joyful smile and the caring of a loving heart and soul.

You have travelled far and long on this road to mastery with its journey of miles and light years, its travails and achievements. Then be still every day and acknowledge who you are, where you have been, and what you can do to express all of your soul talents upon earth.

This soul of yours is a repository of many adventures and learnings, beloved soul, but its greatest knowledge is a compassion for all life, the purity of a nurturing heart, and the joy of creation. This grand universe, expanding as it is, needs your balanced qualities of wisdom and love. You have here on earth those things you call the résumés. May I remind you that you also have cosmic résumés?

DO NOT LEAVE THIS LIFE WITHOUT BALANCING QUALITIES IN ORDER TO ADVANCE BOTH YOUR OWN SOUL AND ALL OF LIFE.

For life you are and life you will be, eternally. When you live it consciously and with loving joy, in as much truth as possible, yet are open to growth and learning, you will never die regardless of the ascension process you attain.The most important thing to tell people today is to love themselves, to love everything, just as the Father/Mother holds life reverently in the bosom of Its own pulsating Lifeforce.

Therefore I say unto you, beloved ones, I, Mi-Ki-el, have been with you before, am with you now, and shall share the transmutable blue flame whenever you need its power during your many excursions in the eternity of existence.

Adoni, Adoni, Adoni...

Chapter 3

Archangel Uriel/Paracelsus

Channeled by Carole Austen

It is I, Uriel, your guide of Liberation, therefore health and freedom, to give input to a planet that is in some darkness. Where you find disease, where you find fear and where you find scorpion energy, you will find Uriel bringing light and liberation to people. It is a pleasure to be with you here again.

Now this grandiose question, "How do the energy cycles of this great and grand universe affect those upon the earth?", opens an interesting discussion. There was a time when, psychologically, those cycles did not affect you because humans upon the earth felt themselves to be the center of the universe.

But today they have discovered that they are not the center of this universe. In fact, the center of the universe is not even visible yet to your astronomers or scientists, or those who give an appearance of knowledge to those who are ignorant.

And so what you have is a pall of fear, of wonderment, and of humans trying to exert themselves to make a mark in the world so that something is measurable. When one feels as if one is nothing, there is little to hold onto. One floats about in the air, unknowingly this way, then that, as if blown by the wind. In matters of cosmic influence on health, for instance, it is very important for people on the earth to feel secure, safe, stable, honored, loved and certainly valued. These issues are a challenge now, which is why you will find great plagues flowing across every land in every direction for no particular reason you can discern.

I wish to speak about the Sun and the Moon in your solar system, for in the Sun and the Moon, and the balance of those two energies, people upon the earth are at definite effect. It is the physical waking and sleeping cycle that you are addressing, and as each body awakens daily it is full of energy, excited by the Sun's warmth, vibration, light and colors that come as a result of the Sun's appearance and disappearance.

All life responds to the Sun's power and people are no different from plants in this effect. In fact, the humans of whom we speak, those "angels upon the earth," have been basically affected from ancient times. For deep in the DNA/RNA structures, a mitochondria, being only a bacteria of sorts in the beginning, still has a bacterial reaction to the earth and the Sun and the Moon as a cycle. In such a time as winter, the cycle is quite different than it is in spring, summer and fall.

Some persons, at a level of conscious intelligence, feel quite uncomfortable should they not go through the seasons, for there are no signals going on in the body to suggest that there is change, appropriate change, nor any instructions as to how to rearrange their consciousness. Your original consciousness is directly connected to, or affected by, the activity of your deepest soul/body remembrance, which is of a plant mind nature.

All cells are connected, of course, both in the physical body and in consciousness, different ones having different organizations and position. However, at one time, you might say they were only "separate" in the nature of a collective community where you have an interrelationship that is essential. If one particular functionality of the mitochondria at the very deepest level is out of sync, then everything else feels at a wondering. Everything else feels discordant, as if something is not right, as if something is lost and therefore must be sought after. It is like a frantic mother looking for a lost child.

The human body today is balanced between the evolutionary history of its many chemical and biorhythmic relationships and the incoming consciousness rate at this time.

For if you plant a beautiful organic plant or flower in a soil that does not support its growth, it shall simply fold and die.

So it is extremely important that those upon the earth create an environment within which those who are new children, those delicate flowers that are the product of imagination, should have a place to sink their roots, spread their flowers and leaves to the sun, and receive the love of those around them. It is essential to heal all humans already on the planet, immediately, so that the maintenance of the physical body during a shift in their genetic DNA structure to higher vibration is achieved.

Much has been given humanity previously about the need for appropriate food, nutritional aspects, and that which is called a breath of fresh air, proper water, purity and so on. Then attend to these matters, please.

Many are now aware that the proper environmental balance must take place within their own physiological level. However, to understand the physiological level, there is the basic creation history to be accepted. The anthropological aspect of medicine has never been considered. In the anthropological development of evolution, you must have certain processes that give the feeling of health, well-being and safety to those individuals who are responsible to be healed and then to raise the new children coming upon the earth at this time.

Ninety percent of human health could be termed as sociological support, and only about 10 per cent is, indeed, what people ingest. A powerful, healthy body can, if given half a chance, maintain itself in joy and happiness. It will, through its own intuition, choose that which is good for itself and bring about true health.

A healthy child chooses for himself or herself that which the body needs to survive. It is known quite clearly in experimental situations that newborn babies given a choice between, let us say, ice cream and cod liver oil, would choose cod liver oil, prior to earthly programming of different opinion.

Understand that the body already knows what is good for it and, if given the opportunity within a psycho-environmental atmosphere of freedom of choice, will create the very best for itself even in people who are older in life years and are undergoing these incoming energy cycles. Whether here already, recently born or about to be born, it is the condition of safety that creates the lack of anxiety in humans.

The basic format for safety on the earth for children now born, for persons who are in mature state, or even for spirits entering into new bodies, then, is essentially the same. This area of which we speak, this anthropological medicine, has to do with three major aspects. Those three major aspects are both practical and in some ways difficult only because of the stubbornness of the human nature.

The first aspect I would like to stress is that of the tribal organization, spoken of by many in recent literature. However, the effects of it are not quite clear to you. When you have a tribal organization and you have a specific place in that tribal organization then you know each day who you relate to and how others relate to you. Then you become networked (your terms) into some functional society in which you have a role that is considered valuable.

Self-worth has to do with tribal organization and your position in it that daily reinforces your good health, and provides caring attention from others. When you have tribal dysfunction, as you do in many situations where people are not coordinated into their basic symbolic mitochondrial awareness, then you have people who feel lost. In the feeling of lostness you have anxiety.

The second condition that is causing difficulty upon the earth at this time is that of gender recognition and of gender responsibility. Few know who they are any more. If they know who they are, they feel safe. If they do not know who they are, they feel unsafe and are uncertain as to their position in life. Again, they are seekers.

So if you have people who are either dominant/submissive or are not certain what their role is as a physical being, they cannot be a role model or have a proper relationship with those around them, new, old or otherwise. And so you have a second contribution to anxiety.

The third anxiety aspect which is causing difficulty for most people on this planet is the division of values created by the evolutionary ancient brain influence. Many people develop a state of anxiety, terror and stress from not belonging anywhere. So they search deeper into their soul for the place of belonging. They experience this place that has not yet been physically located but has been called by many names, such as the subconscious or the unconscious or the other conscious.

This is simply the ancient brain with all its memories of terror and fear and visions of past times when customs and social standards, while they had organization, also contained violent content. So if you have persons who are in cooperative attitudes, they feel quite safe and can experience the world in a cooperative manner. But should these same persons be in a competitive environment, they would find themselves lost, fearful and denied.

And so the third state of anxiety is the "lostness" of those cooperative souls in a competitive environment and the "lostness" of those competitive souls who find themselves in an environment which requires cooperation. When you have these aspects of dysfunction all in a row, which most people have, then you have an environment within which help is not possible. It is essential your technological scientists determine where, indeed, these ancient memories of past lives reside so they can be released and healed!

These ancient memories are contained in the DNA/RNA structure! And these messages are sent through your neuron system to the musculature as well as to the ancient brain, also to the primal, emotional brain and to the higher self. They sometimes avoid the rational mind which is why scientists are not encountering them and cannot account for their presence.

When you investigate people's brains, and put them in a CAT scan, it would be very simple for scientists to make a predictive test in which the same brain areas would fire their neuron systems when ancient memories were being spoken of in a conscious manner. There are those on earth trained in this way. It would be quite simple to arrange such an experiment.

A massive release of ancient genetic memories in humans would usher in an enormously positive healing era desperately needed to relieve human suffering and limitation! We cannot encourage such safe processes, done by caring individuals, urgently enough. You deserve to be well, to become joyful, and to advance as a species as quickly as possible.

Humanity is presently under the power of cosmic and celestial energies to help heal these former limitations and so we will comment on what those physical body impacts are. Also, think what you can do on the conscious level to assist in assimilating those higher energies into physical life. These rhythms and cycles are to make you ready for what some call the ascension process.

On the physical level, some persons receiving these energies experience them as a jolting of the physical body, such as acceleration of the heart, sweating or dryness of the mouth or dryness of the eyes. These persons must turn their attention to the ancient Vedic and yoga practices, or of stretching the physical body and keeping it as limber as possible.

What happens to a person under high stress where there is a new factor taking over an old condition is that a stiffness of the physical body seems apparent, therefore causing anxiety. What you want to understand is that the whole body electric is therefore affected. There are thousands of tracks of electrical current that run through the physical body; therefore, contraction of any of the muscle systems, or tension in the physical body that shuts off these electrical systems, causes them to jam, back up and fill the body with painful experiences.

It is best for these people to swim in water daily to keep their body clear, just as you would ground anything or take electricity off of anything. Water conducts electricity. If we had a way to throw you all into a stream everyday, have you laugh, play games, leap in bounds of joy and health, and laugh at the world in spite of its terrible condition, we would say that would be the best thing to do for the physical body. The hot and cold water changes the electrical organization until such time as the body feels at peace.

The more that you hurry, the harder you work, the more you become stressed. The more pressure you create, the more the electrical energy jams in the physical body. In addition, it is best for you to do deep meditations, have complete relaxation, use music which makes the energies flow in organizational patterns that are pleasurable and keep the body physically fit. In this way you can take the energy changes quite eloquently.

Let us take this a step further and comment upon where the original pattern for DNA appeared in terms of life upon this planet and how the interface or connection with that which is called the space brothers and sisters has had relationship. You must understand that the space brothers and sisters have their own system of structuring DNA and RNA factors in their own physical bodies now, therefore eliminating imperfections.

And so at one time upon the earth we will say that there were many places in which DNA/RNA rearrangements were made by a team of scientists who felt that the properties that were given here on the earth would bring forth a very special being such as yourselves. It was one to two hundred thousand years ago that this experiment was implemented.

At this time, however, we are very unhappy with how some of it has physically turned out, not with the potential but more with the behavioral actions. Thus, it is time again for many of us to contact earth, and to give you information about how to alter the DNA/RNA factors, so that all children are born healthy and with grand intelligence. Should there be an artist available, we could take the factors and draw for you that which you would have to do in order to make these changes. We have brought with us the seed that makes this possible.

Genetic engineering has already begun on your planet and you therefore need guidance. It is extremely important for us to deliver the message that Extraterrestrials (E.T.s) have already done this experience and gone through this same decision-making process which you will enter into within the next months or years to come, very few years.

When you learn to replace all the parts of the physical body and when the scientists can restructure DNA/RNA factors, you can bring forth in birth any kind of human being that you wish. You can choose the color of your eyes, your hair, your skin, your height, your size – all these things can be adjusted. Of course there is a grand issue about what the original plan was and we shall tell you that E.T.s have made all the same mistakes that you are about to make in this area.

You are about to fix the ideal person, and in doing so, you are going to have many ideal persons and you will repeat that factor over and over again. But what will protect you, and protects the entire galaxy, is that we have the original seeds, those things that produce versatility in human development. For only if you maintain a certain number of versatility factors can you always bring forth a healthy hybrid! It is therefore important that your scientists do not think that there was only one original mother/father genetic pattern. There were many!

Most vitally, genetic engineering on your planet needs to be controlled by those who are in a place of altruism, empathy and higher intelligence. They would be those able to accept guidance; therefore, they must also have humility. When you have all of these factors operant, great miracles can be achieved. However, most people on the planet at this time are still in a world that will disappear within a few years anyway.

It is a tragic thing that so much intentional energy goes into this competitive nature. Due to humanity's ignorance and misbeliefs, and their terror at the thought of deviating from the past even when the past was unsuccessful, the majority of earth people are not even ready for the consideration of genetic engineering. And it is not our suggestion that the world even enter into this factor until they have settled those things upon the earth that are yet unsettled and therefore destructive to their broken hearts.

You can understand that even in that which are called the space brother and sister family communities there is the constant expansion within their own capability of greater consciousness and greater wisdom.

Thus, life forms are rather like dancing partners. As that which is grandest comes down into the earth and is received with open arms by those of you who look up to the stars – and who welcome an enhancing E.T. presence – there can be nothing but great partnership.

For those who are still in possession of their territorial natures and are quite satisfied with the fact that they have reached a certain level in life and think that level is all that there is to be achieved, then there is a resistance to E.T. presence. There is always the possibility of sharing and a continuum of relationship with benefit for all, however. Yet, in terms of the fear factor upon your planet caused over the years by the suppression of knowledge regarding the existence of that which is called other life, particularly in western technological societies, there seem to be two groups at work.

There are some who have knowledge about E.T. people and those who know nothing and resist the idea of any kind of intervention from a higher life form of space brother and sister family. Among those who have accepted it, some are in a state of fear because they believe that the energies presently most physical here on earth now are not of the highest quality.

It is true that there are those who are not of the best quality in terms of cooperation with positive planetary objectives. We wish to deal specifically with those stories that you have been told about calculating UFO visitors and affirm there are UFO persons visiting on the earth who are not of humanistic attitude, and have more calculation capability than warmth of heart.

What these people are here for is simply to reestablish their stability and to return to their own universe. They have no long-term particular purpose here, nor are they interested in the human condition. So all factors exist to be discussed. There are those on the planet who will hide, fight or deploy troops against those who are present, should they be detected.

Our intention is to make these purposes so well-known to those who are of a fearful state that they can feel reassured and safe. We intend only the best possible answers for you and for solutions to problems on the earth, which include everyone. We are not just working exclusively with scientists or exclusively with psychiatrists or exclusively with professional people.

We are working with those who are poor, those who are ignorant, those who are imprisoned, and we wish to bring liberation of the spirit as well as health to the physical body. It is for the planet's benefit that we are here, and for all of the people on the planet we bring only love, happiness and joy.

Then let me speak firmly, for we would direct you not to be fearful. There is no reason to be fearful of persons of higher intelligence, even if they are not noted for loving kindness, for they are, at least, rational.

If you are to be fearful, you must be fearful of that which is emerging upon the earth as aggression amongst each other, for you cannot escape aggression amongst each other. It is in everyone's life, bar none, by one projection or another.

It is much more fearful to be an earthling on the earth planet than is to be an E.T. anywhere in the universe now, for there are many malevolent characters on the earth beyond whose nature we have passed many thousand of years ago. It does not serve life in any way to be aggressive with each other. Some of your illusion about E.T.s comes from the Hollywood movies and television pictures of E.T.s out in the universe firing upon each other's vehicles, which is perfectly ridiculous! E.T.s would not even consider such an activity! Space ships are unarmed.

We will tell you that there is no need for aggression, for the unlimited universe has more room in it than can possibly be filled by anyone of higher intelligence. E.T.s do not need to capture planets from each other. They have the facility and technology to create a planet anytime they wish to bring energy together into solid form. It is not that difficult, and you will begin to think in those terms in very short order.

You have large populations on your planet now and you will be displacing both the water, air and energy at a rate faster than possibly can be maintained by your old energy systems. Therefore, you will need help, both in cleaning up your planet and in saving the innocent that are left here, so do not be concerned about extraterrestrial take over.

We will tell you again and again, intelligent people do not harm each other!

There is no need for E.T.s to take samples of your bodies. They have data on you that is non-invasive to your physical body, mind, spirit, or enslaving of your physical nature.

What on earth would E.T.s have you do, should you be slaves? For you would not know how to run anything that is part of the E.T. intelligence system. Everything on a spaceship is run by mind-to-mind contact. Then how could you be useful? Certainly you are a curiosity because there are vague resemblances to those past experiments that E.T.s left upon your earth, and in that way, some of you are E.T. children.

We of the spiritual and angelic realms, and all Masters of Love, wish to save you, whatever your genetic codes, by strengthening your own capabilities and power. It is, however, up to all of you on earth now not to put a burden on any one person to save you.

For any one person taking that burden on must die an early death, either at the hands of violence or at the hands of exhaustion. But more importantly, you must each realize you are your own savior, individually, and in groups. The application of that knowledge is truly cosmic power! All of us are here to help you claim and use it positively.

So it is now time for your vision to be a public affair, a cooperative endeavor. There need to be many more convergences. There need to be many more people who network about the world. This time it is not one savior that must come, but a group intelligence which must wrap the world in another option. With this science of group intelligence, the world can change within it.

Those standing by innocently, and it may even be an advantage they should be blank of mind, can be swept up in this new group idea. You have the facility for communication both globally and intergalactically at this time.

You may receive all the assistance you wish for idea construction and production of new visual images for people, for in despair even the most ignorant will reach for the stars. We can say unequivocally that the human condition is what needs to be addressed, rather than only the environment, but we are concerned about your planet. It is the humans that create it or destroy it according to the nature of their belief system.

Traditional ways of working must change, of course, and new systems of ecological nature must replace the old that bring waste, and therefore a clogging up of the system. The system of Mother Earth is clogged as is the system of those who live upon it. And so a "Good Housekeeping Seal of Approval" is needed here to which we could certainly add some marvelous slogans.

Your country is part of the world which is affected by the media. And you are affected by advertising. Should E.T.s come upon the earth they could not create any great miracles, for there are few of them, but they could give you the information that is needed in order to technically improve conditions upon the earth. But you must somehow create the belief that this is possible, and at the least, implant the belief that new ideas are acceptable.

You have a nation that was built on creative thinking. Can you not bring back these ideas to people? Innovation has brought you great relief from hard labor. Innovation will again bring you great relief from the waste products you have created as a result of your leisure time. Let me give an example for there is always a more divine process.

We have spoken often of a small company that is experienced in the production of different sea lettuces and algae which can, in any desert or warm area, be reproduced every 24 hours in any volume that is needed. These whole green cells that are nutritious and have taken the minerals out of the sea water, which is most valuable to humankind, can be plowed into any field to provide the growing of grand and wondrously healthy vegetables at any time within the year or so of its infusion.

It is a much healthier and simpler process of fertilization than chemicals since every farmer could have his own inexpensive fertilizer-producing plant in the back yard. And it would certainly be a refreshing change from animal and chicken manures which do not in any way enhance the aroma of one's farm.

It is quite economical to have an algae producing operation anywhere in any country and there are several on this planet already that can be viewed. They have many benefits for they can also feed a family of four from the water in a backyard swimming pool. So you can use this material, not just for cows, although cows certainly enjoy it is much as hay and get more out of it than they do their normal feed.

So you would have an organic source of food for the family and the animals, as well as a way to reconstitute the soil and what is grown there. You can grow this algae under very simple, inexpensive conditions. It seems to be a way in which you can replace minerals that are taken from the earth, for these cells replace themselves so quickly that farmers could harvest every day if they wished, and add them to certain fields, reconstituting the entire farm.

You can also take any sort of flowers, if you wished to grow them and waste them in this way, and plow them into the ground, too, for the flowers contain many of the minerals and nutrients that people on the earth need for intelligent thinking. Think back as to when flowers appeared on the earth. Isn't it interesting that intelligence appeared on the earth at the same time? You must look at the relationship between those events of ancient evolution as much as your events in modern times.

Where you are today, in life on earth, is at a crucial junction and we do not need to point that out to you! But there is an interesting experiment you could do that would be quite wondrous and also quite effective. It would be very simple for you to construct a sample environment like most people live in today. Put in present air pollution levels, the ground water and the soil condition which is most depleted, add the vegetables that grow upon it, some vegetation, even some small creatures, some mitochondria, and some cells in this environment. Observe the way they reproduce themselves.

Then take this same cell and put it in an environment of pure air, water and nutrients and see how it reproduces itself in this environment. Since you know that you are constructed of cells that reproduce themselves and old age occurs when those cells cannot reproduce themselves as whole, healthy cells, then you can see the wisdom of giving them the best possible environment! It would be an easy science film or documentary, as you would speak of it, to make.

The project certainly could be constructed very quickly and easily and you would perceive that in four or five generations your own cells in such a polluted environment would be so distorted as to not be able to reproduce at all.

In this way you could see, as we are indicating to you, that the human race may become extinct out of its own ignorance, greed and abusiveness.

But this need not be your fate! We emphasize this statement most urgently. There is more to say, but another speaker wishes to come forth and so I shall depart. May the Creator's energy surround you and lead you ever forward in fruition of the cosmic plan for earth.

And now the illustrious Paracelsus, an early holistic medical healer on your earth, would like to add some personal comments of levity.

This is Paracelsus, speaking in simple terms you can understand, about restructuring your physical body's genetic codes in the New Age. There is a misnomer about the New Age, and since I am really the father of the "New Age" in the medical movement, alive on earth some generations ago, I will say that the New Age is actually an old age. In your recent years, you commonly refer to this as holistic health. Whichever terms are used, I am the one who originated a philosophy of conscious living, which is what this is all about.

There is much vernacular and talk about energies, but in fact if you would change the one word "energies" to "intelligences," then you would find out how everything worked. In other words, what intelligence in the physical body creates a feeling of well-being? Remember that it is a message being sent from one part of the body to the other, and while it is electromagnetic, what it does is register in your consciousness the condition of your thoughts.

In fact, you are the ones who run your energy systems, or send intelligent messages from one part of the body to the other. So you can think of the body as being a collection of intelligent conscious beings interfacing with each other in collaborative activities in order to motivate your physical bodies to do the things they do. In this way, you would interface with those intelligences on a level of conscious activity.

So if you think of everything as being an intelligence, then every single thing has some form or personality with which to relate. For instance, you might have a dyspeptic liver, or you might have a very joyous liver (hopefully it is the latter). In this case you can have a conversation with your liver and say, "How did you like the dinner we had tonight? Are you feeling wonderful?" And your liver would squirt out all these things that it knows to do when you talk to it.

If you think of everything that goes on in the physical body as electrical impulses about which you have a neutral feeling, such as the meridians and so forth, then of course you do not have a personal interaction with your own body.

What you need to know is that you could speak to a meridian and it would curl up and die if you should be angry with it, or it would flow with heavenly grace and sensuous emotion if you invited it to join you in some marvelous practice like stretching or lying on the floor and letting yourself flow in all directions with your emotions.

Think of your emotions as intelligent systems. They give you information all the time. Your body gives you information, therefore it thinks. Your feet and hands think and send messages to the brain. Your back thinks as you lie on the floor. It is registering the nature of the coarseness or fineness of the rug which is holding you up from the wood floor that is hard and most uncomfortable. You could even say to the rug how nice it feels, and have a conversation.

Does it occur to you, for instance, that a pillow has a consciousness, and that you can have a conversation with it? It can have a conversation because it is made of certain molecular vibratory activities that have collected into a form or shape that has its own nature and can therefore communicate with you. Try lying on a hard pillow for half an hour on your bed, and you will understand that you are having a conversation with this creature!

On the other hand, should you find yourself lying upon a down cushion with little soft feathers in it, you could speak to this little goose down pillow and say, "How divine you are, my dear!" And you would get cozier and cozier, and it would fit better and better around your face and your head, and you could sleep in peace and have dreams like you never thought you could have before.

So, in combination, you see, there is a message going back. The pillow tells you that you are loved and comfortable and safe, and therefore you can fantasize divine activities that should keep you sleeping for hours in deep and heavenly dreams.

So don't think you don't have a conversation with just about everything. You are in relationship in life with everything that is around you, whether it is the sky, the chair you are sitting on, your car, a person on the other side of the world, or whatever comes to your mind.

In having conversations with these relationships, you soon discover that everything has an intelligence, especially the rock that gets in your shoe! And you do have a discussion with it. You say, "Get out of here!", do you not? Then you toss the rock away.

So you have personal relationships with everything, and you do communicate, even if it's just an emotion. Let us say you look at it with an evil eye and aggressive intent, and you grab it and throw it somewhere. An action has taken place. You have thought something. The rock has been acted upon and it rolls along the ground to find a comfortable spot in its path. So you see it even has intelligence about where it lies on the earth. It fits perfectly. Otherwise it would continue traveling along the hillside or on the sandy path beneath your feet.

Understand that everything is giving you information and/or altering information because it is an electromagnetic system. It has a personal ability to speak to you in conversation, a dialogue. Therefore, it has a conscious effect on your life and thinking.

If you can accept this, you will have a much more entertaining time through life, and of course if you should apply this to all human beings, then if your liver can converse with you, then Ed's liver does, too! Can you imagine their talking under the table while you are having dinner? And while they are sending electromagnetic impulses to each other, they are definitely having a conversation. So it does help to understand all laws of nature.

And of course, the nature of physics is somewhat the same. Physics is simply a conversation with nature that has gotten so abstract that one can think of it as a mathematical system. A mathematical system has a conversation too. It just does not seem to be as personal as a result of its broad spectrum.

Now let's talk about the spectrum, Light, and the colors in the universe that affect your life and affect the way your electromagnetic energy systems work, whether it turns them on or turns them off. In turning them off, you feel depressed. When they get turned on you feel in the Light.

Of course, when a rainbow appears in the sky you are all in delight, thinking that God has sent you a great gift, and of course that is true. So, knowing that these conscious rises and falls in your life bring colorful people, colorful experiences and joyous interactions into the physical nature will help you to relate in conversations with the consciousness that exists in cells.

The cells vibrate with joy when you have an encounter that you know is going to fill your heart and lift your emotions with warmth from the tip of your toes to the tips of your fingers.

When you make a new friend who can hug you, care for you and treat you with gentleness, kindness and love, you change the nature of the chemistry and messages that are sent from one part of the body to another.

So, if you want a prescription for health, let me tell you that the very best thing is to have a good laugh at least twice a day. You'd be surprised how much that does for the brain cells!

What you want to remember is that your evolution depends entirely on the development of your hormonal structures as well as the development of your higher brain and its dendrite capabilities. In advancing years, you will find that there is a shrinking of these connections, and that is why it takes so long to think of something that you have forgotten.

And so you want to exercise and do some simple things that will affect the pattern refraction in the higher intelligence so that this can get passed on, not necessarily through the body, but through the consciousness. Consciousness is left in the universe by the spirit body to then be picked up by the next generation.

It is not that evolution takes place entirely within the biological body; it also takes place in the spiritual conscious-ness that is now spoken about as a morphogenic field. Con-sequently, you want to leave your highest and most beauti-ful thoughts behind you, for should you incarnate again, you can pick up where you left off. In this way you do not have to start over at the bottom, as in Dante's <u>Purgatory.</u>

You do not have to push the rock to the top of the mountain one more time. You want to start at the top of the mountain, and you want to fly, and this is what you want to teach your young people. Therefore, you should set a good example. I suggest that you practice mental flying once a day in your meditations and see yourself soaring as high as an eagle.

In fact, the pictures or images that you envision make dendrite connections in your higher brain function, and those dendrite connections are indeed important in your concept of yourself. When you think about anything, every cell in the body changes to match the emotion connected to your picture.

That is why it is important for people to have dreams or fantasies of the future, even if they are known as fantasies. They are written down as stories and become mythology or visions of greater potential and capability.

Of course, we could speak with you for hours but that must wait for another time. I only wished you to realize that we who have died the bodily death are not dead at all and also to assure you that there are many definitions of life beyond your ordinary expectations and beliefs. You cannot know how joyous we feel up here when you feel the same love down there that we try to send everyday.

End transmission. Paracelsus.

Chapter 4

'Divine Self'

Joanna Cherry

This material has come to me over the years directly from my divine Self and particular helpers, especially Babaji (the immortal master written of in Autobiography of a Yogi) and St. Germain. I am guided to write it as myself, by offering my mind to God in the writing.

Our History

The first ones of us who came to Earth, to try out having a physical form and to enjoy the beauty of our planet, created our own bodies. We manifested them directly from God light and energy; no birth was required. The physical body then was much lighter, a much faster set of frequencies than it is today. Because we knew we were gods, all-powerful and all-creative, our bodies never aged or died.

We came and went as we pleased, from the earth plane to lighter planes. Anything we desired was instantly manifested to us. We were aware of our oneness with all who seemed separated from us by space. In this heavenly state we lived for a long time. This last part of our history is where the biblical story of Eden, and similar ones in other religions, come from.

The "fall" of humankind came gradually, over many eons, as we began to move away from our knowing of godhood and believe the physical world was the reality, cause unto itself and subject to physical laws only. Beginning to believe we were separate from God, and our thoughts as gods still being all-powerful and all-creative, we began to create the lack and poverty, the disease and war, the aging and death that have been with us ever since.

A deep sense of guilt and fear has also been with us, as we felt the need to create a separate ego in order to feel protected and the ego, to the degree to which we felt afraid, took the place of God for us. And so we have judged this "fall." But even this can be called good and very good, for it has served to objectify – sooner or later – our knowing of our oneness with God.

When we were in that oneness we were in a subjective state, like a fish swimming in water with no idea what water is. We wanted to know all possibilities of life, the difficult as well as the joyous, and so we hopped out of the water - or rather, we believed we hopped out, for our oneness with God is an unchangeable, eternal fact.

Since then, from an infinity of experiences, including going as far as we could into hell, we have been gaining the wisdom that has gradually lead us back toward the water, back into our knowing of oneness. It has been difficult; we have lost much of our sense of love and of power. But to judge our time of apparent separation does not serve us as much as does a loving understanding and acceptance of our decision.

The Illusion of Life-Death Cycles

The perfect diamond of our God-nature has appeared to be covered over by our erroneous beliefs of who we are. As we look around us now, the aberrations of aging, death and limitation have come to be called natural, or at least "what's so" about life that must be borne.

Regarding aging and death: the cycles of nature, the death of animals and trees and the rest, seem to bear out this "naturalness." But human consciousness is the dominant one on our planet; animals and many plants are ruled by our expectation of death. Some trees and plants seem to transcend our consciousness on this: the banyan tree has no known death process, and it seems to me that wildflower plants too must live forever! How many thousands of years do they bloom on the hills, secretly snubbing their buds at the human death credo? There are actually many smaller plants that seem to go on indefinitely.

But by and large, nature has cow-towed to our consciousness. Our belief that the body deceases creates not only aging and death, but the germs and viruses and bugs that harm or kill our bodies and those of animals, and trees and plants. We have even made up internal self-destruct mechanisms such as cancer.

The earth's tilt adds to the illusion of death: many trees lose their leaves in winter, and flowers that can't stand the cold wither away. If Earth were on an even keel, plants and trees everywhere could adapt to an on-going climate and fully express life through all the months of the year, resting only when they chose to.

In reality, it is life that is natural, on-going, expanding life forever! It is we who have made up death.

Coming Home

The good news about us is that, no matter how far we have strayed from our recognition and experience of the truth of ourselves, we have reached the furthest edge of our outward journey, we have turned the corner, and we are coming home!

We are remembering that we are the exact image of God. God as the void, beyond creation, may not have qualities; but as we feel deeply into the underlying nature of life, God expressed in creation, we come upon wondrous "qualities": unconditional eternal love, light, joy, power, beauty, freedom, harmony, peace, all-pervading presence, oneness, eternal expansion, eternal life, perfect wholeness. Really, our one project is to re-experience our oneness with God, our inner divine Self.

As we experience the truth of our mind, we become unlimited thinkers, totally open and allowing of all choice and possibility for ourselves and all others, and infinitely creative. In our feeling nature, we experience our truth as joy, love, delight, abundance, excitement of creativity, the feeling – knowing of power and perfect well-being.

Most definitions of enlightenment stop here. But if we are to go "all the way," to receive the full gifts of our home-coming, it will include the recognition and re-experience of everything as God: mind, feeling, and body.

There is a tendency in spiritual circles to think of the earth plane as "gross physical matter," of the body as dross. "Why be concerned with the body? It is simply a shell, a vehicle we use and discard when we are done with it. We live forever anyway." This is the general argument. But the truth is that virtually all of us are not "done with" a body at the end of a life. That is why we had to invent reincarnation.

It is true that most of our earth lives have been so difficult, because of our acceptance of feeling cut off from God in order to adapt to society, that we badly need a rest, an overview, an understanding of where we've been and where we want to go, in between lives. But the difficulty is not inherent in being in a body or living on earth – it is we who made this a difficult experience. And that is precisely why we need to grace once again this fabulous creation – to experience our body and earth plane as part of God, as paradise.

In creating a physical body from light, we had to slow down light's vibratory frequency until the body could appear solid. The reverse of this process is suggested by Einstein's theory of relativity: $E=MC^2$ is saying, in simplest terms, that when you speed up mass you get energy.

So the physical body is made of light, the primary substance of God. And though it appears solid, it consists entirely of atoms, each of which is more than 99% space. What forms this space into the miracle of a human body is thought, primarily God's thought. (Did we consciously form our own body in our mother's womb?)

Do we consciously carry out the millions of transactions that take place every day to keep us healthy? Do we reform our body as old cells fall away? God's thought is that of perfection expanding: perfect beauty, vitality, health, strength, ever-increasing. It is only our limited thought and feeling that has caused our body to appear to age. Letting go of these limits from mind and heart, and welcoming back our true unlimited God-thought, allows our body to return to its natural perfection.

What happens as we do this is that a quickening takes place: the vibratory frequencies of our mind, feelings and body speed up. It is our ascension process. As the age of light now comes in, everything is lifting, getting faster and lighter, including Earth herself. We are returning to light, to a greater experience of God on every level. We have already learned to integrate light that would have harmed or burned our bodies in the past. Fully accepting spirit through and as our form – God fully embodied – is ecstasy. It is ecstasy we are heading for! And what do we find when we "get there," experience ourselves as light? That we are already there, and always have been. Our true body is the unchanged God thought form for our body. It is our light body, a body which already exists and is here in the same place as our physical body.

Our light body is totally and eternally beautiful; it never ages or dies, never lacks for energy. It is free to come and go through time and space, or rather without reference to time or space. It is age that is the illusion; beauty is the reality. We are learning to tune in to this truth about ourselves, and to express our immortal light body right here on earth.

There are masters written about in many religions who have accomplished immortality, and who have taken their bodies up into light when they were ready to leave the earth. Babaji, the immortal master of the Himalayas written of in Autobiography of a Yogi by Yogananda, is one who is seldom seen outside his snowy realms.

St. Germain, the European mystic, was recorded by various observers over a period of some hundred years to never grow older. These are just two examples. The people who have mastered this process are often called "ascended masters" in the western tradition; "siddhas" in Tibetan Buddhism; the "immortals" in Taoism, and so forth.

Choosing Full Mastery

How then do we experience "full mastery," mastery that includes the body?

The first thing, as always, is to tune in to your inner Self about it. A way to do this that is nearly always accurate is to see how you feel about the prospect of full mastery on earth. Does it stir your soul? Does it excite you, uplift you? Does it give you the feeling of joyous expansion?

If it does, you can be assured that your inner Presence is saying to you, "Yes! This is God's desire for you now. Give it your energy!" If it doesn't move you, there are probably higher priorities for you right now. But your mastery is unfolding for you, and the kind we speak of here is coming for you in your right time and way.

If you feel unclear, it can help to go into a deep meditation space with your inner Self, picture yourself as a full master, and see what happens.

If you are guided to give your energy to this process, you will want to stay attuned with your inner Self about it each day, for you will have your own way to come into full mastery. It may be good for you to practice the methods given toward the end of this chapter, or you may want to modify or discard them, as suits your own way of growth.

Rejuvenation: Physical Level

Let us look at the regeneration of our bodies from the ground up. On the "purely physical" level, are you following what is most loving for your body? Are you eating what feels most right for you at this time? Foods are all thought forms just like our body, and we have the ability to transform any food – with our thought, love, light, intention – to a frequency that is totally beneficial to our body. This includes coffee, chocolate, Twinkies, etc.

But until we fully empower ourselves in this ability, our body will love some foods more than others. Raw and organic fruits and vegetables, soaked nuts and sprouted seeds and beans hold the greatest natural light. But there's no judgment on any food, including meat; try and just listen to your spirit and the highest desire for your body, and follow that. Many wonderful new substances are available today also that can enliven and lift your body.

Are you giving your body movement of some kind that it wants and enjoys? Are you giving it light, at least in warm weather? Are you giving it loving touch, hugs, pleasure? If sexual fulfillment is a desire of your heart, are you allowing that in your life?

Sex deserves a special mention. Many spiritual teachers hold that sex – especially for a man – is weakening and aging to the body.

But there is a higher truth about sex, which is that when it is practiced in the context of the whole being as a divine act of love, an equal exchange of energy, and the raising of the sexual energy through the chakras to the crown of the head, it can bring the whole being into ecstasy and is a powerful tool for enlightenment.

How about your breath? Do you breathe deeply and freely? Do you allow the life force in the air to nurture and sustain you? Once in an ascended state, I felt the air around me to be so vibrantly alive, so loving, it seemed that just to breathe it would rejuvenate my body. It is good to invite in and accept the qualities we want from the air.

This usually means a shift in our mind and emotions, which is true of the acceptance of all physical-level blessings, because nothing is "purely physical." The physical plane is a manifestation of thought and feeling. It comes from our spirit and our mind.

Rejuvenation: Emotional Level

On the emotional level, assisting our body into immortality means clearing out unresolved issues, many of which can be held for lifetimes in the muscles and cells of our body, where they create tension, density, and often illness. We need most to forgive – to forgive totally ourselves, all others present and past, and all events and circumstances.

Often, forgiveness must be preceded by the release of anger, fear, or guilt. Body work is often a wonderful tool to release old emotion. There exists now an amazing variety of body work to choose from.

A vital part of clearing emotionally is giving up the set of feelings we have held, subconsciously and consciously, around aging and death. I have heard that in Africa, if a member of a certain tribe is condemned to death by the elders, he sits down under a tree and wills his own death within 24 hours. Imagine the sense of self betrayal and the suppression of joy that takes place in us following our mandate to die, very slowly!

We have become so used to feeling this, although it is usually unacknowledged by our conscious awareness, that it has been like adjusting to carrying a 100 pound backpack so that we say "Weight? What weight?" Clearing this emotional set that becomes so soaked-in to all levels of our outer being is a great challenge – but what a blessing to let it go!

One of the tools of emotion that is very helpful to our body is simply to love it. The judgments we have placed upon it are felt and responded to; reversing them to love and honor our body brings the body joy and upliftment and light, and is a vital part of a regeneration process.

Rejuvenation: Mental Level

On the mental level, bringing forth immortality means releasing all the ingrained limiting beliefs about our body and replacing them with the unlimited truth.

There are additional understandings which can be helpful to include in the new mental construct about our body. The chakras, or seven major energy centers of the body, are vital to a regeneration process. These centers spin, and the rate at which they spin, and their rates of speed relative to one another, are directly involved in how young and alive a body is.

A slowing down of the spinning takes place after puberty, and consequent aging. The spin can be speeded up again by knowing it needs to be done and creating the intention that it will be done. There is a fine book that is helpful to this process called The Ancient Secret of the Fountain of Youth, by Peter Kelder (Harbor Press). I differ with it only regarding sex.

The ductless glands that are associated with the chakras are also "called to duty" for the regeneration process. The pituitary gland, or master gland, associated with the crown chakra at the top of the head, is the most vital of these. After puberty, by our command that the body age, the pituitary begins to produce a death hormone.

It also instructs the other glands to comply: the pineal

with the "third eye" chakra, the thyroid with the throat chakra, the thymus with the heart chakra, the adrenals with the solar plexus, the pancreas with the abdomen, and the reproductive glands (ovaries or testes) with the root chakra. We can awaken these glands to their true work, which is to cooperate lovingly and joyously with a regeneration process!

Personal Experiences with Rejuvenation

I would like to briefly share my own experience with rejuvenation, as I feel it gives this writing more believability and weight, and thus allows it to be a greater gift.

When I first discovered that regeneration was possible, I entered into 'youthing' projects with great excitement and enthusiasm. And they worked – for a time. I saw change, and others consistently let me know it was working, though I hadn't told them.

But always I came to a stopping place. I seemed to have no power against it. As this happened again and again, I became discouraged and apathetic about youthing, and stopped trying.

Finally, in the fall of '89, I was able to see that there was a wall that had been stopping me, a barrier formed of specific thoughts of some kind.

I became lion-hearted toward this wall. In meditation I flew across green fields toward this low, black wall and when I got to it, I flew directly into it. Inside, I noticed round black thought forms and I flew into them. I realized they were fears of death I didn't know I had.

As I dived into them, they blew up into space – nothingness. They disappeared! Over a period of weeks, I flew back into the wall a number of times, until I experienced everything as clear.

In the fall of 1990, another great breakthrough occurred when I was led to directly and passionately address my pituitary gland. I thanked it for producing the death hormone in the past, as I had asked it to.

I told it I had remembered that I was an unlimited God, and desired to regenerate my body. I commanded it to stop producing the death hormone immediately, and begin to produce a life hormone.

Well! The whole top of my head opened up, and light poured in. My pituitary was in ecstasy. It communicated to me, "Thank God I no longer have to do what was onerous to me. I can do my real job now!" Since then I have learned more about the other glands and have been guided in how to do a complete regeneration.

You will find processes below that have been vital to my understanding and experience of regeneration. It is helpful to go into a state where you feel as close as possible with your divine Self: centered, calm, strong, loving and loved.

Dissolving Barriers to Rejuvenation

There are some common thought/feeling barriers that come up for people as we move toward rejuvenation and transcendence of death. Here they are, with truth "antidotes" to help you move through them. You may want to say these aloud, with certainty and passion.

1. Rejuvenation cannot work. Both aging and death are certain.

Truth: Beauty and perfect health are already my reality. Rejuvenation – the healing of age – is as natural as the healing of a scratch. Death and aging are unnatural. As God I Am, I have all the love, light, power, knowing, determination, and patience I need to succeed in my rejuvenation.

2. I fear aging/death so much that I inexorably attract it to myself.

Truth: There is nothing to fear about aging. I am totally lovable no matter how my face and body look. I heal fears of aging through God I Am.

There is nothing to fear in death. If I chose to die I would go into the light and be lovingly welcomed by my beloved divine Self and loved ones who have passed over. I would be completely taken care of and would move into good new experiences. Through God I Am I heal all fears about death.

3. I don't deserve the good of rejuvenation.

Truth: I am a beloved and totally innocent being who has always done my best, every moment, with what I had truly learned. God created me innocent forever, and nothing I have ever done or ever could do can change my innocence. I have never in truth harmed anyone, because each person is a whole and eternal God-being, who co-created with me our perfect growth and highest good for that time. I forgive myself completely. I accept that I Am as God created me.

4. I am not safe to be different. I will be abused or killed by people who do not understand. (This is a past lives experience of many of us.)

Truth: I heal all past lives through God I Am. I am safe, completely protected by my divine Presence and any other masters I call upon. I am safe and loved in the world, lovingly supported by all people in my rejuvenation and transcendence of death.

5. I won't be loved. I'll have no friends. I'll be outcast from society.

Truth: Many people have already done this, and many more are doing it now. My friends may not be my old friends or family, but I will have wonderful friends – we will find each other!

6. If I rejuvenate and transcend death, I will betray my family and friends who have aged and died. Loving them means doing as they do.

Truth: The most loving thing I can do for my family and friends is to show them by my example that they are all powerful and beloved gods who can rejuvenate and transcend death.

7. If I rejuvenate, I will become trapped on earth.

Truth: By the same process of my rejuvenation – becoming one with God I Am in my experience – I also learn to take my body up into light, so that I may leave Earth when it is right for me. I can even go back and forth between the earth plane and lighter planes.

8. If time changes for me/if my body changes, I won't know who I am, how to define myself.

Truth: I Am eternal now. I Am God I Am. This definition of myself transcends any other, and I accept it now.

You are likely to have all of these thought forms to some degree, as they have been virtually universal in our culture. Regarding any of them, the way out is thought. Pick one that it feels right for you to release now. Call upon your I Am Presence or a favorite master to be with you, go through it with you. Gather your lion-heartedness. Fly or slip into it. Feel it, but continue moving through, deeper and deeper. Here it can get complex: you may find that the one issue is breaking down into two or more. If this happens, you will want to repeat this process with each one.

This is fine; just pick one of them and begin to move through it. If you really do this, you will find it blowing up into space, or that you have come to an outer edge of the form and space is beyond. Leap into this space! Now let the form fall away beneath you, or rise above it until it looks very small below you. Say to yourself, "I created that." Really get that you are the god who created it. Get it all the way into your belly. Now add, "And it's okay that I created it." Feel that too.

Now, see that the only reason it exists is because you put it there. Each day you have chosen to give it your creative energy, so that it would continue to exist. When you withdraw your energy, it can exist no longer. Do you want to do this, to un-create it?

If so, choose how you want to do it. I thank it first, thank it for serving me, and invite its energy to go into my new creation. Then I picture a big red electrical switch, that has been up in the "on" position. Taking both hands up above my head, I throw the switch downward, simultaneously saying "Kaboom!" I see the form below shrink into a pinpoint and then explode into light.

Now, what is your new creation going to be? Refer to the truth antidote for your thought form and let it assist you. In forming the new creation, feel it, enjoy it, accept it deeply. Give it your energy over the following weeks (or months or years) until it becomes real for you, until it becomes "the way it is."

If you find the old form returning, recognize that it is still serving you in some way, and try to feel what that is. This work often peels the issue away in layers. When you feel ready, repeat this process. It is an extremely powerful one, the best I have ever used for dissolving something no longer wanted and creating what is wanted.

The following processes are designed to be spoken, aloud if possible, with great clarity and passion. You can also make a tape of them and play them back to yourself when you are either awake or asleep.

Release of Death

Do the un-create part of the process just described, going into your thought/feeling about death. Here again, you may find a number of different ones to go through. Frightening past life deaths often come up here; and the terror around the belief that you can cease to exist. You may want to work with these issues for several days or longer to clear them or begin to clear them.

I forgive myself for ever thinking and believing that I was separate from God my source, and for all the lack and limitation experiences that have been born from that original thought. I forgive myself for ever creating death in my past, or aging, illness, or limitation of any kind in my experience. I know that I was doing the best I could do with what I understood at all times, so I do not judge myself for the experiences which were created from limited thought.

I now give up death. I give up all aging of the body, all illness, and any other effect that limited thought has had upon my physical form. I give up the idea of being any age. I Am ageless and eternal. I give up attachment to being "one of the crowd" in pretending that this light form must die. I give up all emotional attachments to death and dying in every form, not only in my body but in my mind and feelings as well. I give up funerals, funeral parlors, and grave sites. I give up the idea of leaving life. I joyously accept eternal aliveness now! (Take time and let this soak in.)

I know that I Am one with God. I Am the wondrous being that expresses as myself. I Am the light. I Am the love, the joy, the power, the wisdom and all-knowingness, the freedom, the unlimitedness, the perfection of my real self. I Am the ever-expanding life.

I now allow and invite this perfection to begin to express fully in every area of my life: my mind with unlimited and truthful thinking; my natural feelings of love and joy; and my body with its rejuvenation and renewed perfection, its healing from any appearance of illness – its expression as the divine substance it is!

My body is everlasting life, wholeness and perfection. It is God in expression, now and forever. I live in this body as long as I desire on earth – I can live a thousand or two thousand years if I wish – in ever-increasing beauty, strength, health, aliveness and joy. When I am ready to leave the earth plane, I take my body up into light, so that no body remains behind. I am thankful for this truth of my being. And so be it.

It is a good idea, if you want to fully release death and aging and accept your aliveness, to give patience and persistence to this effort. An absolute belief does not die easily, especially on the subconscious level. What is a decade or two, if it takes that, compared with the eons we have bowed to the "last enemy?"

You may need time to face and move completely through fears and beliefs you have held about death into the light of your being. But you will find that the courage with which you face them is the same energy that frees your life expression: increased aliveness and joy are the direct results of this work. Ask you inner self to guide you in this process, and you will move through it in the way and in the time that is perfect for you.

Clearing the Subconscious for Life

Beloved subconscious mind: I love you and thank you for helping create the death process in the past. I know you have thought you were protecting me. You have been serving me perfectly.

I want you to know that I've changed my mind. I have

remembered who I Am, an unlimited god. I choose to live, not to die. I choose to rejuvenate my body. We are safe (an overriding concern of the subconscious) to rejuvenate. I ask you to cooperate in this. Will you?

Look into your deep feelings now and see if you can feel how your subconscious is responding. Allow it to be honest – this is a huge step and it cannot be forced.

It may be saying "Huh?" or "No way." "I need more information." "I'm thinking about it," or "Let's do it!" are other possible responses. It wants to cooperate, but you are likely to need patience and perseverance to get your subconscious mind's full support.

Once it aligns with your rejuvenation process, however, your success is practically guaranteed.

Reversing the Death Hormone in the Pituitary

My beloved pituitary gland! I thank you and acknowledge you for producing a death hormone in the past, as I requested you to do from my belief in death.

I want you to know that I have remembered who I Am. I Am an unlimited god. I have realized that death and aging are not real. I choose to rejuvenate this body.

I lovingly command you to cease now to produce the death hormone and begin to produce a life hormone!

I further charge you to awaken all the other glands to joyous, ongoing cooperation in this regeneration process. I thank you!

Let this sink in. Envision the stopping of the death hormone. See and feel the life hormone begin to flood your body. Feel it enlivening every gland and organ, every bone and muscle, every cell and atom of your body. Feel your body's response!

It is good to repeat this a number of times to prevent yourself from falling back into your old way of being, and to allow the new way to become rooted and strong. When you repeat it, change the words so that you are thanking your pituitary for continuing to leave behind the death hormone and to produce the life hormone.

Your Light Body

To your subconscious mind all imagined events are real, so visualization can give you experiences that quicken your mastery.

Visualize how you want to look. For that is probably what you really look like in your light body, your body of perfect youth, health and beauty, infinite energy and aliveness. That body is yours now. It is the way your physical body was intended to look, and the way it would look if you had never believed the limited thoughts of our culture.

You can ask your I Am Self to give you a vision of this beautiful body, or imagine what it looks like. See it clearly (this often comes piecemeal rather than all at once), and when you are ready, step into it.

Now feel the light essence of your body. It may feel as though you have no organs, or that they have nothing to do. It may feel totally harmonious, stress-free. See each atom radiating the God-light that is its reality, in each area of your body.

Allow this light to increase in brilliance, and realize that this brilliant light is the God-thought for your body. See its light shining through and actually absorbing the physical body, transmuting all into the true perfection of your God Self. Take time and enjoy the experience of being light, your true essence.

Patience is good to have in this process. It is good to ignore the mirror and see your light body shining through the physical, which may continue to age for a time. But if there is a true acceptance of your oneness with your God Self and all the goodness that includes, at some point your light body will become your manifest body on earth.

A Rejuvenation Program

This has two parts: a meditation and an action.

I. Meditation

Go into a meditation. Feel centered and grounded. Breathe deeply and gently. Relax your whole body, part by part. Become detached toward your mind. Relax your feelings. Bless your whole outer being.

With each chakra:

Open it (see and feel it open).

Fill it with light, radiating infinitely.

Awaken (or affirm the awakeness of) the glands associated with it, seeing it joyously and fully cooperating in your regeneration process.

Spin the chakra faster, to optimum speed (clockwise) or affirm its continued optimum speed.

The chakras and their glands:

crown	pituitary
third eye	pineal
throat	thyroid
heart	thymus
solar plexus	adrenals
abdomen	pancreas
root	ovaries/testes

Feel and see your body as God's body. Say and feel things like, "This is God's body. God formed this body, and God is reforming it this moment. Without God, I would have no body. God's will, energy, love, intelligence and life are running this body right now, taking care of everything."

God expresses its perfection through and as this body. This is God's heartbeat. This is God's breath. This is God's liver, God's kidneys, God's organs, God's glands, God's bones, God's muscles, God's immune system, God's eyes (etc.).

"I give up my old way of defining this body. I give up my old way of looking."

"This body is regenerating/rejuvenating now. I put God/my divine Self to work in every atom of my body, to create success in this process. This body is transforming into my perfect light body, more and more every day. My muscles are (or are becoming) strong. My skin is smooth and clear, my face and neck are young. My eyes are perfect (etc.)."

Visualize your perfect light body. Step into it and feel it. Become it. Give yourself some time and feel this as completely as you can.

Resolve that while this transformation is happening, you pay no attention to your mirror, give no power to appearances of age, no power even to the process not seeming to work.

Remember that what you give your attention to, mentally and emotionally, must manifest. If it seems to take a while – though it doesn't need to take long to start showing – so be it.

II. Action

Follow the daily program to do the five or six Tibetan rites (physical exercises) from The Ancient Secret of the Fountain of Youth. Before beginning each day, you may say, "I give thanks for this program. I honor it. I am attuned with those who have greatly benefited from these rites. We do them together." Then as you do them, feel and see them working perfectly for you.

As you finish at the end of your day, you may say, "I place my divine Self in complete charge of my rejuvenation. It continues all day today, all night tonight, and into the following days, weeks, months and years, as long as I choose. I give thanks for it. So be it."

If, after a time of your best effort, you feel nothing happening, it means you are blocking success in some way. Check the section on common thought/feeling barriers, form a true intent to clear yourself, and go to work on them.

If you begin to feel you are forcing yourself with the process, take a break. Put all work and all rest in the context of eventual success, and it will indeed come for you.

All blessings to you in this endeavor!

Chapter 5

Hilarion

Channeled by Jon Fox

Greetings to all of you. This is that energy-being or vibration you call Hilarion. Before beginning with the topic at hand, we will remind you of the idea of energy as used to connect to you. You could imagine it as an emerald light extending from infinity upwards through all of you down to the center of the earth, and you are in the midst of this beautiful energy.

It is that which is clearing, cleansing, valuable, beneficial, but see it also as that which allows you to release into the earth ideas, expectations and denials that may be within you and holding you back from these simple truths we wish to present to you.

This topic, "The end of disease on planet Earth," is a grand title if there ever was one. You are all aware of this topic deeply within you. Many of you have come to this planet to witness this change. It is not inevitable, but it is more than possible.

It is contained within you genetically to understand the nature of disease in the first place. The intent of our willingness to speak with you about this topic and to share the information is to articulate several facets.

First, to allow an awareness of this possibility within you on a personal level to your way of thinking, of feeling, of sensing. The end of disease on Earth is not a fluffy fantasy or a diversion. This is a truth, a possibility, a reality. This is something that you can really know.

Second, we wish to provoke you to search for, discover and use that which is unique and special in you, to bring this into form. For after all, that is what we are about – provoking or helping people in some way, pushing them along or sometimes just reminding them that they are in material form to learn about the material world for the purpose of bringing form into action, into reality.

Third, and perhaps most important, to recognize with you that the purpose of disease on Earth, much more than having an intellectual purpose, has to do with love, and is a way of understanding your fellow men and women, all of the other kingdoms you share on planet Earth (the kingdoms of the animals, the plants, the air, the Earth herself) and of course the spiritual orders, the devic orders, the nature spirits and so on.

The point of this is that you begin to recognize that from the purpose of disease comes an entire understanding of life that you already have, though you have yet to bring it into full consciousness. By choosing to become more conscious of the fullness of life within you and around you, you complete the learning cycle in a very deep and real way, and you need the disease aspects no longer.

If any one of these points brings you a deeper understanding of disease, then we have been successful; but more importantly, you have been successful because you do not have to have empirical evidence for this. It is simply an observation, from our vantage point, of what you are here to learn from disease, among many other things.

Each time you get sick, each time there is something out of balance within you, there is a lesson or something previously unknown and unconscious now coming to the surface.

That the imbalance shows up as disease in your physical body indicates that your being has had no other way to remind you of this, and has not been able to share this view through your emotions or your thought processes or dreams. Many of these may have come first.

Many of these may have reminded you, and you have not heard or listened or learned for some reason. It could be just too much stress, too much to do. It could be it is a very important lesson from a past life incarnation. It could be because the knowledge of this confronts your understanding of yourself and you would have to change in a way you do not consciously welcome in order to accept and learn the lesson.

Whatever the reason, what usually occurs in this process is that the body, by some means, reveals to you that it is out of balance. The body is indicating a problem: something it feels is wrong.

At that moment, at the very first understanding of this, take the time, energy, effort or whatever it takes to learn the purpose of the imbalance and why this is coming into you. Not why at the cellular level, at the genetic level, at the disease level, at the scientific level – those are all very nice and very important, but well-covered by others. Instead, learn in yourself what the purpose of the imbalance means to you.

You will generally come up against a wall of resistance of some kind. An important principle to recognize here is that the potential within you equals the resistance that you come up against multiplied by that which you allow to flow in the world.

Potential equals resistance times flow.

That means that if this resistance is there, you know there is also a potential waiting to come through. You will note in this that the potential will manifest subtly in the symbols that are directly associated with the disease.

Your body and all its various component parts and interrelated systems serves you as a symbol. (We have spoken of this extensively through another channel in the book called Body Signs, which you may wish to consider.)

By way of an example, look in yourself to a time when you had a little twinge of pain in the knee. Recognize this as symbolizing a way of showing you the combining of the earthly (represented by the lower leg), the emotional and the physical, with that of the more spiritual aspects in your life (represented by the upper leg), which include the mental as well as an understanding of higher reality or the higher self.

The integration of this is symbolized by the knee. You can avert the knee problem when the twinge begins by taking the time to absorb that lesson of integration and by looking actively in your life for such a thing.

This sounds very simplistic when applied to the great difficult diseases, like cancer, AIDS and many others. Here you can recognize a pattern, often of denial, which is more complicated. This has gone on, sometimes in only one lifetime. You have attracted the disease to you by some means and, in this lifetime, you are unwilling to look at the lesson; this becomes then the source of the resistance and further denial.

Denial is a funny thing, you know. It puts you into position where you don't see it's there. The denial tends to cover itself up. Yet as you look and as you meditate on it, as you ask for dreams about it, little inspirations will come.

One of the reasons you have attracted disease into your life will come to you. You can then ask for help. You can get help from your friends through their opinions and sometimes their ideas.

If you do a therapy that is holistic, that changes the cellular structure, that brings the inherent healing abilities out, then these ideas will come more quickly. Antibiotics or vaccinations or things that do not accelerate the inner healing process are less productive than those things that *naturally* accelerate your own processes of inner healing. The denial will present itself and you will be able to deal with it more easily.

This does not guarantee cure because, in so many individuals, there is a very powerful lesson to learn. It is a pattern that they have dealt with in many lifetimes, and it is possible for intervention to come here at a physical level.

This intervention could be doctors, healers and others, but you must understand that the reason they are drawn to do their work is not just because of making money or willingness to help in the general sense. You will be drawn to that healer, and they to you, to exchange life lessons.

That healer will have something to learn from you, as well as you from them. You can remember your own value when you come to a healer saying, "You are my last hope. You are to help me. I can do nothing for myself." This attitude is useful because it allows you to surrender and usually tends to dissipate the denial.

However, it sometimes keeps you away from seeing your own uniqueness, your own truth, your own love. As you go deeper into this, you may begin to recognize that there are many solutions.

Those of you who are the helpers and healers can similarly keep in mind that in order to help others you need to remember the need you have to heal yourselves. How many of you are perfect in your body, your mind, your soul, your spirit, all the way through? We aren't just snibbling over details here, because there is within you the idea of this perfection and you can come to it.

Yes, you must heal yourself as you heal others. The trouble is if you look really bad, people aren't going to trust you. They are going to say, "Well, if he can't heal himself even to get rid of that baldness or that particular skin condition or his obesity, how can he possibly help me to do that?"

Present to your client the specifics that we have mentioned: that you are here not only as the healer to project a healing energy, or to use technology appropriately, but also to counsel and to help them understand within themselves the reason they have attracted this.

You can then say with total honesty, "I am struggling with a particular life lesson myself, and that is why I manifest these particular symptoms that you are seeing in me. It is not an excuse, it is simply the truth as to who I am."

If then, by example, you are able to reveal some of your own life process, your life lesson, the universal law that you are dealing with, this deeper level of understanding and revealment in your process, you can set an example for that person and actually make it better for them. And so it is good, deeply good that you have something to work at in yourself, for then you have something to use as an example.

Is that too simple? You must understand that the flip side of this, not just that you counsel them but that they counsel you, is also there. And some of those you work with will be brought to you because they actually have something of value for your little problem or your big problem, whatever it is. What they are there to share with you may have a lot to do with your path.

Unless there is some way in which the vibrations of

your two souls can come into harmony and resonance for at least a moment or two, there will be no healing.

And those other people, the ones with whom you can't come into vibrational resonance, are the ones who leave you and say, "I don't like that person; I'll go somewhere else."

The reason you can come into this place of resonance is that your souls have a similarity; you are connected. You have a vibration to share between you. This bridge will be there with every being that you are able to help at all. Sometimes it is necessary, though this sounds absurd, to ask for it from them! "Now that we have dealt with these things, and you've paid me (or you've received the healing or whatever), perhaps there is something you have to tell me. I don't know what it is but perhaps you do?"

Even some statement like that can be quite provocative and helpful in what you do. So, we ask you to work with that question, from the general and into the specific. It is a way to bring the uniqueness of everyone into form, and it will assist you in discovering new options.

These new options and solutions to various very difficult health problems have been with humanity now for only a short time, a matter of about fifty years or so. Your society, as a mirror or a "reflection" of your inner attitude, has suppressed these inventions, these ideas, these technological shifts.

This suppression takes place for several reasons – the obvious one being greed, as well as an unwillingness to accept change, and also your dealings with power and darkness and light and all the usual battles that are brought into form by so many of you. There is another reason that is a much grander part of this plan.

It is the essential core of our topic today: *Is humanity as a whole ready to let go of the path of disease as a path of learning?*

This question cannot be answered simply with an, "Oh yes, I think so," unless that is coming from all of your being, your soul, your past lives, the core of you, your essence. It is humanity's very nature in accelerating and knowing that essence that it reaches out to all of humanity. And so then, this becomes very much a societal issue, even a political issue, if you wish to examine that.

The interesting thing about this is that your society is now amidst a great deal of change. It is coming to new ways of recognizing and working with the negative thought forms that would say these ancient ways of healing, now made anew, are not to be used. Instead, your society is saying: let us look at these possibilities. Let us examine them and let us dismantle the institutions that are holding onto the aspects of resistance and denial to these new technologies. Let us dismantle them and change them.

But, when you have a disease and believe that the technological solution is your only solution (which as we have already said it is not), then you may feel quite desperate, even quite angry at these institutions. You are not easily able to see that their understanding of you and your condition is a reflection of <u>you</u> in some way.

Are we suggesting that it is time to forgive the Food and Drug Administration, the American Medical Association, the American Cancer Society, the National Cancer Institute? Should you necessarily forgive many of these organizations that have a role to play in suppressing what is new, and a public relations policy to promote <u>their</u> ideas rather than these new ideas?

No, but forgive them in **yourself** – the part of you that would in some way say, "I am not willing to accept a new idea from someone. I am not willing to examine my own level of denial or resistance."

This is very important, not so much for the people who are struggling with difficult illness, but for the **healthy** majority, because they are the ones who are setting policy. They are the ones reflecting their own vision and ideas, and that includes many of you here.

Then would we be saying that we are calling for a change in these institutions and how they reject and change how these new ideas come into form? Yes, but the change comes from within you first. And from this way, it is actually possible to forgive these organizations.

To understand the story and history of institutional suppression from a purely technological point of view, we would certainly suggest you study or examine the books <u>The</u>

Healing of Cancer and its companion, The Cancer Cure that Worked, both by Barry Lynes. These books show the story in a new way, as a whole endeavor.

Taking on the medical establishment and challenging these institutions as a whole is not the only way to bring change to your society and to begin letting go of disease. The "business" of disease and healing can be made "personal" by you and you can yourselves become the models teaching a way of service.

Business as we perceive it and understand it, as we have detailed in the book Vision, is a rather artificial set of things. You utilize money in order to signify some way of giving and receiving, of sharing your love in the world. Might it be a little simpler to do this directly? Because there is something that you really love to do, you do it in the world and there is someone else who loves to do what they want to do and they do it for you. Sounds very Utopian, doesn't it? How is it going to pay the bills? Well, under such circumstances there aren't any bills.

Simply understand within yourself then that it is possible to change this reality. In the meantime, you are stuck in the middle. You are between the two worlds: that of the old way in which the money was utilized as a substitute for love and that which is the new way of service.

So you have to 'make do' with it as fits your own personality, as you can accept. If you can only accept charging a certain amount for a service, then that is what you work with, and somehow you then come into alignment within this in yourself.

We have extensively commented on this in the tape now called "Meaningful Work: Money, Service, Love," and we refer you to this, both audio and video versions. They are sort of fun to look at because they stimulate this aspect of how you see for yourself that which is perfect for your own being, which will be different than for someone else.

For as you are healers, you have to pay your bills too and you have to understand the balance of this with others, and this is definitely important. The process will also show you a spiritual aspect of yourself because the money as representing love, even though it is by the old way, the Piscean way, it still is a truth for you and that truth must be accepted as it is appropriate.

Let us look at this deeper issue of disease as it comes into your life. It brings to you the inner life lesson and offers the knowledge of your being. You are required to change. Sometimes the change does not look very good when you start.

If you then ask, "Where is the part of <u>me</u> in this? Where is my essence in this? Where is love in this?" Look for something that you honor, that you find important in your life, and say, "Where is this that I hold important?" As this answer is revealed to you, you are then presented with the first handle to take hold of this life lesson and bring it to you.

In the case of cancer, if you learn that life lesson only to the level of fifty percent (meaning that you understand it and create it in your life essentially half the time, in half of your consciousness, with half of that which is important to you), the cancer will move into remission. There are many cases of this. Of course the doctors have wonderful names for it, but in yourself, you are different when you accept that inner lesson.

Then ask yourself, if you would create that much suffering for yourself, that much struggle, what kind of an energy is your soul? Is this a horrible over-shadowing force saying: "We are going to make him sick in order to make him learn," or is this perhaps only one side of the truth?

Maybe the soul is saying: "I love this being so much that I will do everything within my power to project this lesson, this love, this understanding, this awareness into that being." That is the soul's job, when you separate from the soul and come into incarnation.

Oh yes, that separation is there. You will have contact with the essential soul energy from time to time, but to always have it with you, well this is called enlightenment. In the state of enlightenment, many things are possible including spontaneous healing, the end of disease and the way in which this is ended for others.

But there is more, there is also within you the merging of potential and flow and the end of resistance. For disease represents resistance in your life. It is really that simple.

As you come into deeper and deeper contact with this lesson of disease and you become more aware of its essential core and you change as a result, you then must face usually one very clear, very deep issue.

This is what you will notice in your friends who struggle with cancer, and it is the part that you cannot talk to them about. It is the part in yourself where the denial runs the thickest and it usually has something to do with loving yourself, with recognition of God within your being, with an acceptance of the higher self as an important part of who you are. That is the lesson of your soul and you as one.

Before you incarnated, you decided that among the other things you would know would be this inner knowledge, this love, this way of helping, this way of loving. That is what you are here for. Some of you come here to work out the karma (meaning the cause from a past life manifested now as an effect with the disease in this life), specifically to balance and create this energy that then allows you to notice love.

Usually this is the hardest part in dealing with the deeply denied issues around difficult chronic diseases, because you come up against it and cannot accept it at its magnificence.

To lead you in a little meditation will assist. We would like you to think for a moment of someone who has an illness (not yourself, please, although at a later time, when you are more practiced with this technique, you can do it with a second image of yourself).

Think of somebody who has some difficult disease, something they are struggling with – someone you care about. Allow your breathing to become easy and steady. Imagine a beautiful, full light as if from infinitely upwards, pouring down into you. Give it a beautiful color – perhaps a golden light, an emerald light, a silvery light, a beautiful white light. Let this energy move through you and stimulate you, helping you to be this higher self that you know within you.

Rise up into this light in your imagination and from this high vantage point, held within this beautiful light, look down on your friend who is struggling. Ask within yourself, "What is this person's uniqueness?" Let an answer come into your consciousness to reveal some specialness of that being.

Now, recognize that from our vantage point, this is how we see every one of you. You each have this specialness, this uniqueness, this special way of being on earth which is so different from everyone else, and you are very much able to contribute and share this with others.

If you can remind your friend of this now, energetically by your vibration, by your love, you will actually usually have greater impact than if you can tell them about it in person. So now, imagine in your heart the same colored light forming itself into a beautiful ball of energy, and in your mind's eye or physically, you extend your arms and let that beautiful ball of light energy now move out to your friend.

Holding the vision that you have of their uniqueness, transmit it to them lovingly, as if you are saying not just, "I love you," but, "I honor you; I honor the specialness in your being." Now return to your physical body. Come back into consciousness here, and be aware of the room.

This is a little portal thing. It is to shift attitude, not to create dramatic energy change, but for some of you who really do care about your friend and do recognize this specialty in them, you will indeed be contributing to their lives.

Next is the greater question: Why then would one wish to incarnate? To balance or just so you can become a better person, just so you can learn more or make more money in this world or perhaps have more friends?

No, nothing like this. In fact it is so that you can appreciate and understand the oneness of the cosmos, perhaps that is your unique life path.

Perhaps you incarnate to understand in some deep way what it is to be. Perhaps it is to know in yourself enlightenment or the way of God; or perhaps it is some way in yourself in which you wish to see a form of the creative urge, creative understanding as something magnificent added to your world so that earth herself is made better for it.

These are grand schemes. Because they are so grand on a galactic scale, they must revolve in time with the principle of universal principle, universal law, universal understanding.

We have detailed this extensively in our little book called Vision. And the understanding of this book is that there are these twelve universal principles, each of them relating to your manifestation here, and that, then, is the real secret to disease on earth.

Understand that, with disease, there is within you a universal principle that has been disobeyed, that has been somehow neglected, that has been denied or perhaps (and this is really more common) you are aware of it. Perhaps you are aware of the energy within it. Perhaps you do not want to yield to it and be one with it.

The use of the term "universal law" has some connotations within it that are very difficult. It sounds a lot like the edicts as to how you are to behave, dress, act in your society and all of that nonsense.

However, what we speak of goes to a much higher dimension, plane of existence and understanding at the soul level. Universal law is understood and held throughout the universe by beings on all dimensional levels.

Some of the universal laws such as the Law of Opposite Expression (a thing and its opposite tend to be created together and work together and be allowed in form together) will not show themselves in an obvious way in other parts of the universe. You do not have to have healthy people living beside diseased people.

This is because the Law of Opposite Expression, under some of these other societies who have understood this, then relates primarily to the understanding of light and darkness, and in their society they have chosen light and allowed darkness to be on other worlds.

For instance, some of this darkness is around here, as you have noticed on earth. In yourself, you have these universal principles embedded in cellular memory.

They are absolutely necessary for the incarnation in the first place. They are the principles by which a form or idea comes into a physical form in the body, in the life, in the reality around you.

As you balance and come into contact with these universal laws, experiencing them within yourselves, playing with them, understanding them, you may suddenly notice in your life an acceleration of karma. Things happen a little faster. Many of you are already experiencing this.

You don't have words for it such as, "I happen to be working with the Law of Opposite Expression," or the Law of Karma or the Law of Reflection (**as above, so below**), but you will understand that as you approach this actively, you actually prevent disease in the first place.

This is a very hard concept to understand because it is really so simple. It is the way by which you actively seek out and work on these universal principles. It is fine to do this intellectually by considering how in your life you are not obeying this principle or this other one. It is a fine thing to begin this way, but you will find within you that the <u>real crux of the matter is in the emotions</u>.

There is a part of you unwilling at some level to accept and, ultimately, to actively manifest one of these universal laws. This is very hard to understand within you. You would say, "I wish very much to help my planet, to share my life with others, to help people," and so on, but look carefully.

You may not be using the Law of Help deeply within you because you are not willing to ask for help. Somehow, deep within you, you are going to do it yourself, by hook or by crook.

With every universal law, there is some inner emotional principle that will usually hold you back from a deep understanding of it. This has been repeated in lifetime after lifetime. It is the feeling sense, the emotions, the heart sense that continues from lifetime to lifetime.

Sometimes, an example can be quite helpful for you in coming to understand these universal principles. Let us assume that a client or a friend may come to you speaking of a problem with a fibroid uterine tumor. She is dealing with her acceptance of the entire reproductive system and what it means.

The fibroid tumor has generally been benign. Science feels it unnecessary to operate, unless of course there is great pain, excessive menses or other difficulties. This condition represents a blockage to the reproductive and creative force.

Usually, the individual would deny some level of sexuality allowed to move through her as a functioning way of expressing herself in the world. We are not talking about becoming a stripper or a prostitute; we are referring to the way the individual expresses the fullness of her creativity.

That same part that is regenerative, generating life in the world, bringing this sense of beauty and love that might be similar to a child, is an energy not willing to be shared with the entire physical body.

As an example of the life lesson, this individual may have come often into this reality to understand the universal principle that has to do with the Law of Love, which connects all things together like a glue. There is also somewhere within them an unwillingness to accept the Law of Reflection, which recognizes the body is a reflection of what is deeper in their own hearts or their own souls: **as above, so below; as within, so without.**

Those are two universal principles that often come into action. Usually, it will take a third principle to bring this into physical form and that is the uniqueness of the approach of that person and their own particular gifts.

In the case of this individual, it may have to do with the Law of Permanence, or willingness to recognize incarnation, to accept this, to say, "Yes, I am." The "I am" principle is often recognized in spiritual literature as very important. To know it within yourself and to really understand it is a nonverbal experience. This is not something that you can pick up and read about in a book.

As you search for the answer as what to do and utilize the technologies that are now becoming available, the technologies developed by the individuals Royal R. Rife, Gaston Naessens, even Wilhelm Reich, and many of those wonderful and powerful nutritional therapies now coming into action, you will find many solutions – even just eating a raw beet with its oxalic acid content to dissolve fibroids anywhere in the body.

But if these techniques can reveal (as if from the cells outward) some of these denials, these ways of holding back the energy, then the person has made a true step forward and the healing holds.

The new technologies that are now coming into form will handle the diseases for you at the physical level, but you will not have learned the lessons within them unless you actively seek them out. As we perceive it, these new technologies will be made available first to the healers who are able to promote within you the idea of looking at the universal principles, releasing the denials to the life lesson and coming to know the beingness that you truly are.

Thus the healer becomes the counselor, and the counselor becomes the healer. In this way, you are your own best healer and your own best counselor.

It is now time to reveal the secret agenda of this little talk in the first place, which by now most of you have realized. Within you, ask the question: are you ready, do you wish, can you accept it, is there some way within you now willing to let go of disease as a path for learning on Earth, and see this release among your brothers and sisters?

At first, the question is an obvious one and it is easy to answer; and then you recognize the real truth of it and how deep it goes into your core and it's not so easy.

We ask you to recognize it again from the higher vantage point and if the answer is even a little bit of a pipsqueak of a "yes," you will find that these possibilities reveal themselves.

They are all around you now to be revealed, and then the shift really occurs, where you accept on some deep level that this can be a part of your existence.

You have not been taught this, you know. Many of your mothers said to you, "Don't go outside without that particular article of clothing because you are going to catch a cold." That incident becomes your association with catching a cold, and there are deep issues about this to be resolved within you, most of them dealing with your own patterning.

In some of you, the aetheric light bulb is already beginning to blink over your head as you recognize that little pipsqueak of a "yes" that is the real "yes," not the "of course" yes, but the "soul" yes – the one that says, "Yes, it is time," and "Yes, I love myself enough to allow this."

And for this, we honor every one of you. As you open to the emerald light now within yourself, we will allow it into you to the greatest extent possible.

For this moment now, we ask you to accept within yourself for just a moment, the idea that disease has ended on Earth. Try it out and see how it feels. Pretty simple, isn't it?

But imagine that at the moment there is this idea that your soul has something to tell you and you are not willing to listen, something happens in you. It is warm, beautiful and loving, and a light falls upon you. A sense of caring for yourself forms the words, "I am willing to listen, I love myself, I sense and know this God within." Something like that is felt within you, and then you just listen. That is how it would work, that is how it is working now if you listen.

In the advanced meditation form, the visualization which we mentioned earlier with the light within, see a second image of yourself. See what comes, what it wants to be told, what is being held as an image within it.

See this in yourself and know it. These little things prevent disease and can help you understand a little more of why you have come here to understand this.

This does not mean that you should certainly give up all of the other techniques and tools, but use them in combining and knowing all of these other things, and disease is ended on earth. That is our perception of it, and you are at a crossroads. If the answer to "Are you ready?" is: "Yes!" then you have taken the fork in the road that will lead inevitably to the end of disease on this Earth.

We are most grateful for your willingness to hear these ideas, to receive our love, to look inside yourselves for all of this and to understand these principles of balance and disease at a higher level.

We encourage you to seek out more information and go further with this within yourself. You may find it is a tremendous source of inspiration and energy from within you – and for this we are most grateful.

Chapter 6

IXACA

*Coordinator of the Council of Twelve of Interraithe, a vision-
ary planet in the Orion Constellation; Quetzalcoatl of the Mayan
Culture; Elijah, the Prophet; and Imhotep of Egypt.*

Channeled by Verlaine Crawford

1. The Planet Earth was created out of the same fiery
mass, the same light source that created all physical matter.
It is the process of the Source to create, to send forth energy
which solidifies into form. Therefore, this planet emerged
from the Infinite Knowing as an orb coalesced in the magnetic circumference of your star, the sun.

The Earth, in the way that you know it, is more than just
a rock with a molten center. **Earth is the Library of all Life
forms in the local neighborhood of Galaxies.** The Earth has
been planted and pruned by the Gardeners who roam this
particular area of the Cosmos. The distance from the sun,
the rotation and the ability of the planet to bring forth life
have helped it to serve as this elegant garden where various
plants, animals and levels of consciousness of human kind
may reside.

All who have taken form are Points of Consciousness
assuming that particular formation for a period of time. Time
serves as the reference point in dimensional travel.

It is that point when the rain drop touches the Earth and
transforms itself into nourishment. It is the point when the
Consciousness of All That Is touches the Earth and transforms itself into a myriad of forms.

Each of you capable of reading these words and contemplating this message is a Human Being. **Hue = Color; Man = Manifestation; Being = Light. You are Color Manifesting in Light.** Imagine a rubber ball filled with light. Then imagine puncturing holes in the rubber ball, millions of holes. Each one of you is one of those holes with light flooding through you. You are Points of Consciousness of All That Is.

As a Point of Consciousness of the God Force, you have always been and always will be. You exist in All Time, All Dimensions, All Space. Your Consciousness is now focused into this particular time and space, yet you are not limited to this arena.

It is similar to your focusing this moment on this particular page and on this particular WORD. If you expand your vision, you are able to see the edge of the book. If you expand further, you see your hands holding the book, and then where you are sitting, the room around you or the garden. You are able to see the furniture, the trees.

If you look out the window or up through the trees, you see the sky. What have you done? You have expanded your consciousness, your awareness.

Why did you choose to take form, to live on this Planet at this time? Because You, the creator, enjoy becoming one with creation. Your evolution as a Point of Consciousness has been to move through all of creation, to experience all levels of density and to live through each moment of the creative process.

You are far greater than your body, which you created out of the atoms and molecules which respond to the seed thought you brought with you, far greater than your emotions, which you use as tools or creation (Emotion = Energy in Motion), far greater than your mind, which you use as a forming device for Inspiration.

You are Spiritual Beings expanding your consciousness (awareness) to encompass all of life.

The actual process of creation of the human form has been through experimentation with countless varieties of life forms. Nearly every form of animated life (animals) that exist on your planet have evolved into thinking, communicating beings on various planets throughout the galaxies. This planet, Earth, has served as a nursery and a library for those life forms.

Mankind, as the evolved life form of Earth, decided to serve as caretaker, to have dominion (not domination) of the planet. You chose to use your love (the glue of the Universe) to keep a harmonious atmosphere, so that life could continue to evolve.

As you well know, after entering form, many on the planet began to forget their heritage as spiritual creators and began to identify with form. They began to believe that they were separate from creation, rather than the flowering of it. And thus fear was born.

Love is the glue, fear is the chaos. Love holds the atoms and molecules together, it is the creative force. Fear breaks the bond, it separates, and thus causes the chaos and disintegration of the physicality.

This 'fear scenario' is one way to create growth. Think of yourselves in terms of soil in a garden. You are the nutrients, the humus, the ground out of which plants may be grown. You, as soil, have been baking in the sun. You have become hardened and feel separate from the sky.

You have retreated under a shell and hold yourself back from interacting with All That Is. Now if you break the ground, if you create the furrows in the soil, it is possible to plant the new seeds which will spring forth and unite you with the sun and sky.

You, as Spiritual Beings, immersed yourselves in the density of matter. You experienced the feelings of separateness. You danced in the dreams of death and destruction. You lived in the shadow of the hate and misunderstanding. You are now breaking apart the old structure of belief. You are planting the seeds that will transcend these many centuries of fear-based experience.

Your evolutionary path is to expand beyond the density and at the same time to use the understanding (to stand under) of all that you have gone through. To truly understand that the concept of separateness in the cause of all dis-ease and the continuous fighting through all of the centuries.

You and your planet are now moving toward a birthing,

a birthing of Global Consciousness. For in the past 5,000 years, you have been passing through a beam of light, an acceleration beam, and you have 20 years left to travel through this particular light. The acceleration beam is similar to your Gulf Stream in the Atlantic Ocean. It is a natural phenomena in this Galactic neighborhood. Many planets have moved through this beam and have risen from the density of the third dimension into fourth and fifth dimensional frequencies.

The Earth is moving through a birthing, and the consciousness of all life forms is being accelerated into greater awareness. When you have been born (Being in the Light), you will move forth as a unified consciousness individually and as a group. You will join with beings throughout the Galaxy that have achieved this expanded awareness.

2. The DNA/RNA codes are understood by your scientists at the same level that they understand the Galaxy and its complexity.

As you look out into the night sky with a high-powered telescope in your observatories, it is obvious that the billions of stars visible and invisible are arranged in patterns and clusters. If you were to decide that you could decode the universe by deciphering the patterns of the galaxies, you might entertain the idea that you could thus understand creation.

The same is true when you look inward at the nature of the cell. You have 26 letters in your alphabet, and are able to construct millions of words in a variety of languages from those few designs that you call letters.

The letters and sounds of those letters have no meaning in themselves, yet you arrange them symbolically on the page and utter them with your voice and gather meaning from those sounds and pictures.

The "alphabet" of the cell, the DNA, has over 100,000 instructions! 100,000 compared to 26! To imagine the complexity and variety that can be orchestrated from such a diverse design is nearly impossible for the human mind in its current state of awareness.

You, as Spiritual Beings, are the architects of this body in which you reside. It is your thought forms, your core beliefs, held in your auric field, your Soul Essence, that has brought you again and again and again into physical body.

Yes, there is a code, but the code serves as the instrument, the piano, the flute. YOU are the player of that instrument and you play the same tune for a lifetime. It is only when you get tired of the tune that you begin to lose energy, that you begin to wither and die.

The Acceleration Beam through which the Planet is passing is raising the vibrational frequency of your body at this time. Imagine a blender filled with milk, fruit and protein mix. The ingredients are sitting in the blender. They are relaxed and settled into their appropriate level, either at the bottom or floating near the top.

Now, you turn on the blender. The ingredients begin to turn and move against each other. You can watch the show as they toss and turn as the speed increases. Eventually they blend into one another. In the end there is no separation.

The Acceleration beam is the blender. All that has been separate within you is being turned and mixed. You are seeing past thoughts and emotions coming to the surface. You are experiencing events that remind you of memories you thought were long forgotten. You are facing your fears in living color.

What holds your body together in the midst of all this change and confusion? In the blender, it was the milk serving as the base into which the fruit and protein could blend. In you it is the Love, the love of you, that serves as the base into which the emotions and the experiences can blend.

True health is coming into agreement with you, just as you are today.

So be in the blender. Love every part of you, especially the areas that you don't like, especially the problem areas, for Love is far greater than just saying, "I like you." Love is truly the glue that holds the cells, the atoms and molecules, the DNA of your system together. Love is the field out of which you grow. If you dislike any part of you, you begin the disintegration process.

It is very important to understand the Chakra system. These Wheels of Life, these Vortexes of Energy which animate your being. They have been called Chakras in your

Eastern tradition.

The Chakras are the connectors to the full Soul Essence of you, which resembles an Oval of Light, similar to a large egg, which expands out beyond your physical body by approximately three to five feet. Each Vortex is a receiver and transmitter of electro-magnetic patterns of energy.

Each Vortex (Chakra) corresponds to a level of consciousness (awareness) and serves as the "channel" for that energy, for that thought form, to enter the system. At the base of the spine is the Survival Chakra. Most of the time, you are not concerned with the basic ingredients of survival; breathing, digesting your food, organizing the functions of the various life-giving processes of the physical body.

Yet, when you concentrate on thoughts of fear and death, disease and destruction, you are interfering with and confusing the natural flow of energy of the Survival Chakra.

The second Chakra, located below the belly button, is the Sexual/Creative Chakra. This area of your life, this Vortex of energy, would normally be very natural and not need much conscious thought.

Sex, procreation and creative expression are essentially an experience of the body and physical life. Yet your societies have made this natural process into a moral issue. So it is that guilt, fear, repression, resentment, confusion and self-hate have thus established a blocking of the flow of life into the Sexual Chakra.

The third Chakra, located in the Solar Plexus, is the inner sun. It is a center out of which the flow of life comes animated and activated through will and power. The desire to accomplish, to bring forth into form, is moved through this Vortex and out into the world. Thoughts of fear, powerlessness and confusion stop this solar power from energizing your inner thoughts into form.

The fourth Chakra sits in the center of the chest. It is the Heart Chakra and serves as the Vortex through which moves Love, the glue of the Universe. It is the Fourth-Dimensional experience of the Emotions (Energy in Motion).

The Heart Chakra serves as a centering position between the three Chakras of spiritual reception above the heart and the three Chakras below of earthly expression. It is the Vortex through which thoughts begin the process of taking form.

Tiny patterns of electrified thought packets arrive at the Heart Chakra and become animated with the glue that holds all creative expression together. Thoughts of sadness, separateness, self-hate and fear stop the gluing process.

The fifth Chakra, located in the throat, is the Communications Chakra, the next level of creative expression. The Throat Chakra represents what you consider to be the "thinking mind."

It is the fifth-dimensional experience of being in thought, the Mental or Etheric Realm. The Communications Chakra takes the ideas presented through inspiration and organizes these insights into cohesive concepts.

Thoughts of unworthiness, fear, stupidity and aggression stop the flow of inspiration and paralyze the Communications Chakra, resulting in mis-communication and disorder.

The sixth Chakra, located in the center of the forehead, has been called the third eye, because it provides insight (seeing between dimensions), intuition (inner knowledge) and psychic ability (seeing what cannot be seen with physical eyes).

This **Psychic Chakra** takes inspiration and begins to show the recipient a snapshot of a possibility. It serves as a center between spirit and creation. Fear of the unknown, the unseen, the unheard restructure the Psychic Chakra and cause feelings of separateness, misunderstanding and loss of self-worth.

The seventh Chakra is located at the crown of the head and is called the Crown Chakra, the thousand-petaled lotus. It is the highest frequency receiver of All That Is and becomes the entry point for knowledge beyond the known. The Crown Chakra receives inspiration (in Spiritos/in Spirit) directly.

It allows the recipient to open completely to the God Force, the Soul Essence, the Higher Self and experience the Peace which passes all understanding. Thoughts of unworthiness, lack of deserving, fear of life and death restrict the flow of the Source of All Power.

True health is relaxing into the natural flow of the Vortexes of energy that animate the physical body.

Relax. Relax. To be lax. To allow the mind, the muscles, the energy of life to go lax, and then to re-lax. Your subconscious mind is simply a tool to see, hear, feel and communicate with the physical world.

Ninety per cent of the activity of life is not controlled by the conscious mind. Yet the conscious mind can interfere and cause dis-ease. So, relax.

3. Heredity is the continuous reproduction of the genetic code established through the thought pattern of generations of similar thinking, thus imprinted upon the matter that is condensed in physical form.

Each individual Point of Consciousness chooses the genetic interaction appropriate to the thought patterns manifested in the soul body. The physical body is then adjusted to the thoughts and to the past-life experiences of the occupant.

You might compare heredity to different types of automobiles. You have a type of design called Chevrolet, Ford, Honda, etc. The genetic code compares to the machinery designed to shape each style of auto. They come out of the factory essentially similar, except for a shape of a fender, the headlights, the length of the chassis, etc.

Thus, you have specific ethnic groups that have their own particular shape of head, eyes, torso. And there is the possibility that, after you buy the car, you can customize it. You can change the design, and yet it will usually retain the essential ingredients that made it a particular model. The same is true of your own occupation of the physical body. You can customize the unit, and you do.

Environmental influences are a direct result of the thought patterns that you receive from your particular society. You begin to customize according to the conditions of those around you. Often your customizing is the result of fear and confusion, and you begin to remodel the body to serve as a protection, rather than an expression of life.

The basic factors of heredity and environment remain constant. The increase in the vibrationary field is simply activating and showing the "mind" the thoughts that it holds.

It is no longer possible to be oblivious to what you are thinking. Thus, as you change your thoughts, the physical body will follow suit and begin to react in a more healthy manner as you clear and clean your consciousness and examine "core beliefs."

A major "Core Belief" that affects all of your lives adversely is the belief in physical death.

From the time you are old enough to understand the language of your society, you are told that you must die. It hangs around you, this concept of death. It tracks you; it's behind every corner. You live in constant, unconscious fear of death. This could be a helpful belief IF it created an atmosphere in which you dove into life totally and 'lived in the now' completely. A few people do react that way and live full-out, enjoying their lives.

The majority of people react to this belief in physical death by living partially, breathing shallowly, loving a little, barely moving into the body, for fear of being moved out quickly. The idea, the outrageous concept that you could have physical immortality, that you could live forever may seem ridiculous. However, we suggest that it is imperative to change this core belief as you move into the higher dimensional frequencies.

Imagine that what we say is true, that you and your planet have moved into the Fourth Dimension as of April, 1990. Fourth dimension is the Astral Realm. It is the frequency range that in the past was the area you emerged into when you passed from physical body. You have entered the Astral, therefore you have died and are not aware of it, because the entire planet went with you. How can you know that this has happened? Look at how time has speeded up. Look at how quickly your thoughts become reality.

Now that you are in Fourth Dimension, you now have the opportunity to consciously choose any age you want for your physical body and to experience the health and vitality of that age. You may take this same physical body with you to the next dimension, the fifth dimension, the Etheric, or Mental Plane, as the Planet moves into higher and higher frequency.

With this concept of Physical Immortality, you might then say,

"You mean I could keep this body through all of time?" **Yes.**

"Oh, my, I guess I had better pay attention to my body!" **Yes.**

"Really?" **Yes.**

4. Each individual is a microcosm of the macrocosm of All That Is. You are a hologram of the God Force that animates All. Have you ever seen a hologram lasered onto a sheet of glass? It becomes very three-dimensional. You can look at it from many sides. Did you know that if you break the glass, the total image is, incredibly, on every piece of glass? You are that piece. You are the total image.

Cosmic cycles and rhythms are similar to those exhibited in all living things, and every thing is alive. The structure of the tiniest cell mimics the rhythms of the most complex organism. The Universe is alive. It breathes in and out. It moves into form and passes into non-physicality over millennia. Over 90 per cent of the universe is invisible, just as over 90 per cent of your awareness is unconscious.

There have been Big Bangs, as in your theories, and they continue through all of time. There are Black Holes, as you call them, that move energy through dimensions and twist in upon themselves to form mirror images and parallel Universes. That is the macrocosm of your experience of moving through dimensions and experiencing parallel lives.

Throughout all dimensions and through all physical representations, the same flow of energy, the movement of creativity and chaos, the yin and the yang of All That Is moves unabated, perpetual, without beginning or end.

5. As the dimensional shift continues and you ride the waves of energy moving across your planet, it is important to take time to relax and open to the spiritual flow, to meditate as you call it. Morning and evening to sit and quiet the mind, to move beyond thought into that realm of light and peace. The reason for meditating regularly is to give the mind and body the habit, the ritual, the experience of peace. Then you will find that this ability to become quiet,

to move into center is with you always, all ways. You will slow down time and enter timelessness. There will be time between sentences, between words, because the mind will not be chattering away at you. It will learn to be quiet.

Begin by imagining that you are a large lake. See rings in the lake, similar to the rings in a tree. Start at the edges of the lake and begin to smooth the water. See it becoming even and quiet and watch as it becomes like a mirror, reflecting the trees around the lake. Smooth the next ring, coming closer to your body, and the next and the next until you see all around you a calm lake, smooth like a mirror.

Now move into the body and continue smoothing the energy deeper and deeper until you reach a center in the center of your chest, in your **Heart Chakra**, in the center of the Pyramid (the fire within) where a small flame flickers and glows. Move into the flame. Slowly, easily, expand the flame upward and move it through your throat, your forehead, up through the Crown Chakra and out of the top of your head as a fountain of energy.

Follow the flame downward, gently back into the heart and now expand the flame down into the solar plexus, into the Sexual Chakra, into the base of the spine, and out through a grounding cord into the earth.

Expand and expand until the flame reaches the center of the earth. Move your consciousness back up through the flame, into the body and stop at a point just below the belly button. Stay there. Relax. Breathe into your belly. Relax. Breathe. Stay there, concentrating on your breath. Be in that place of your birth, be at your connection with All That Is. Relax and breathe.

Your ability to stay in the body and to realize (real eyes) that you can see all of life and can change all of your circumstances...all of your problems, by going inside, by seeing that life is a biofeedback system.

Life is showing you who you are and what you are thinking. Life is the mirror for you to see you.

Until you realize this fact, this law of creation, then you will continue to experience the feeling of victimhood, the feeling of pain and frustration, especially as the planet's energy is being shaken, as you are being turned upside down, similar to a wine bottle with sediment at the bottom. You are seeing the sediment. In order to clear away the debris, you need to be quiet and relax.

6. The energy in your bodies is the electromagnetic field that moves the pulsations of thought forms into the field of density that you call life and "reality."

The pulsation is consistent with the creative force of all things. It is the Consciousness of You that moves the energy or blocks the energy to various points within the body.

As the field of density lightens, your thought forms must also lighten, or they will disrupt the electromagnetic field and cause disease and decay in the physical body. You can compare this change of thought to the creative effort of chiseling stone for a sculpture.

One needs heavy instruments, a hammer and chisel to break away the fragments to reveal the shape within. If you use those same heavy instruments on clay, you will create a large mess.

Chisel and hammer on clay will simply break apart the substance and chaos will result, no form will emerge. So you use your hands to model the clay. Gently you form the image, often adding to the clay, rather than chipping away.

If you are working with liquid, for instance Jell-O®, you mix the ingredients and then pour it into a mold, and you let the cold of refrigeration harden the liquid into form.

As the density lightens in your environment, you are moving from the hardness of stone to the lightness of the liquid.

The method for creating form must change to accommodate the new material. Therefore, your thoughts feeding your emotions must change. Thoughts of rigidity and separateness, of fear and hate, of pain and sadness, need to give way to flexibility and oneness, love and nurturing, joy and celebration.

On the physical level, it is important to change your diets and lighten the foods that you eat. The animals of the planet are going through the same transformation that you are, and their systems are toxic with the change of frequency. Therefore, it is suggested that you feed off plants that are receiving energy directly from the sun. The fruits and vegetables, grains and greens that provide nutrients directly to the body are the source of life for your systems.

Packaged vitamins and minerals must be watched carefully, for the body will reject that which it cannot assimilate. Avoid processed foods, sugars and artificial ingredients. Eat of the natural nutrients provided in the *living* plants. Drink deeply of fresh water, and breathe down into your belly, and you will create a healthy body. **Which minerals draw you to them? You may find that these are lacking in your diet and you need them for healing.**

Gems and crystals have within their energy field healing and disruptive influences. **Pay attention to which ones you are drawn to.** The presence of these lovely creations helps to lighten the heart and changes the thought processes.

If you allow yourself to meditate upon the wisdom held within the crystals, you will come in contact with the totality of existence, for they hold the mystery of growth and the synergy of design.

Each of you is moving from a carbon-based pattern to a silicon-based design. You are becoming crystals, the Christ incarnate, the receivers and transmitters of the energy, the presence, the infinite knowledge of All That Is.

7. As there are many relationships between individuals, your family, friends, work associates, passers-by on the street, so are there infinite numbers of relationships between the space brethren and spiritual masters who have served physically on the planet.

All of the spiritual masters have served on Earth and on other planets. All of the human beings on this planet have had experience on other planets. For some, Earth is the place of origin. Their first experience in human form with an open awareness was on Earth.

The majority of Earthlings have had their first experience in form elsewhere in the Universe, usually in the local neighborhood of Galaxies, which includes billions of suns.

Those who have emerged as teachers on Earth are those who have not forgotten who they are as they became immersed in density. They were able to awaken and know their origins and tried over their lifetime to awaken those who could listen. Not everyone would listen, as you have noticed.

The Angelic Realm is indeed the sixth dimension, the Spiritual Realm. (Seventh dimension is All That Is. We are describing the Universe in terms of Seven Dimensions, and there are gradations of these dimensions that others have called separate dimensions. The terminology limits the grand sweep of layers upon layers of interrelated dimensional spheres.)

Those who have opened their consciousness to a wider view, beyond thought, beyond time, beyond space, are said to reside on sixth dimension.

When you speak of the governmental relationship with certain UFO forces on the planet at this moment, it is important to define governmental and UFO forces. Governmental is far too broad a term, for you have millions of people working for the government who only have their families and retirement uppermost in their minds. They have only heard of UFOs in the tabloids in their local supermarkets.

There is no governmental conspiracy. There are a few people who work for private agencies associated with your government who have knowledge of extraterrestrial spacecraft. There are an even smaller number of people who have been working with E.T.s to develop a project to help the planet in its progress toward transformation.

UFOs (Unidentified Flying Objects) is a misnomer. The majority of objects that are intergalactic spacecraft are easily identifiable. There are a variety of visitors from all over the galaxy visiting Planet Earth during this transformation. The majority of beings are at a level of consciousness that is beyond tampering with or endangering the species now incarnate on the planet.

There are a few Fourth and Fifth Dimensional beings, who have not opened their consciousness to a level beyond thought and have not tapped into the Infinite Source of all wisdom. These beings still contemplate the **knock-em, sock-em** mode of interaction. They are being re-educated as to the nature of their function, and the need for caution has been emphasized.

Those who would cause disruption and pain on this

planet, whether they be born to physicality on Earth or else-where, are currently being escorted from the area. Very large friendly forces, several millions strong, are currently within and outside your solar system. They are here to clear the way for the enlightenment of the species.

Those who would control, disrupt or destroy the planet will be experiencing the acceleration shift and will be ren-dered helpless in their own soup of pain and fear.

As we have stated, each of you has the ability to clear your energy field and to open to a new reality of thought, feeling and action. You are the creators of your life.

If you buy into the conspiracy scenario, you are con-tinuing the thoughtform of victimhood. With your endless stories of conspiracy, you are taking office politics into the cosmos.

Yes, it is prudent to be aware of all facets of life on the planet and elsewhere. Yes, there will probably always be those who prefer the dichotomy of love and fear, pain and pleasure, joy and sadness.

What we are suggesting is that you are the decision-maker, you are the one who decides which thoughts you will entertain, which thoughts you will hold in consciousness. As the decider, the creator of your reality, you will then send forth into the Universe the thought that will take form.

So if you want to think about conspiracy, you will create it. If you want to think about evil empires, you will create them. Just look for a moment at the Soviet Union. It wasn't that long ago that the majority of people in the U.S. believed that the Soviet Union was an evil empire.

What do you see now? Many, many changes!

8. The Gulf War, Desert Storm as you called it, was a physical demonstration of the Astral Realm, the Fourth Di-mension, where emotion rules all. Hussein and Bush each represented to their followers an example of "good against evil."

Each stood as the outer manifestation of the inner war that is raging within the people of the world.

Saddam Hussein provided the Earth with an experience of Global Consciousness. All the world voted to hate Saddam.

He entered Kuwait just one month after your planet had moved into Fourth Dimensional Frequency.

Thoughts must become reality. Thoughts with emotion (energy in motion) behind them will become reality faster and more clearly.

You manifest what you desire.
You manifest what you fear!

The greatest desire on the planet was for the end of the cold war between the U.S. and the Soviet Union. Through economic considerations and bankruptcy of the superpowers, you were able to put down your guard and find that you could negotiate a peace.

The greatest fear on the planet was that, even if the Soviet Union and the U.S. were able to come to terms, a madman might arise (probably in the Middle East) and threaten the entire world with nuclear capability.

Voilà...*Saddam Hussein!*

You manifest what you desire and you manifest what you fear. **The only way to change the insanity on this planet is to understand that you are the creators of it.** As you turn your consciousness inward, realize that you have thoughts of power and control.

Realize that you would love to stand tall, to be remembered by the entire world. Recognize that you, too, might have within you a desire to eliminate all that oppose you. Move inside and begin to dialogue with all parts of your being. See that these parts of you are being reflected to you in extreme in your life, in your newspapers and on your television.

Begin to converse with these different parts of you and ask if there might be another way to solve your problems. Perhaps a way different from anger and fear, frustration and battlement? Would these parts of you be willing to change?

What if you could accomplish the same goals without all of these arguments? What if you could live happily and peacefully and still have the things you want? Would these parts of you be willing to change? It starts with you.

You are the creator of the leaders who represent you. You are the creator of the protagonists who continue to show up in your life. **Create a new interior and a new exterior will emerge.**

9. As the library for all life forms in the local neighborhood of galaxies, this planet is in need of a reorganization. It has become jumbled by the confusion in the minds of humans.

Without love in the hearts of men and women, the devas and elementals are working overtime to try to save the lives of the plants and animals. They need the creative force of love from humans, for the disintegrating force of your hatred has nearly destroyed the planet.

Unless you change your minds, there is little that can be done by those E.T.s and Spiritual Masters residing on and visiting the planet. We have come as Cosmic Consultants. We cannot and do not want to take over this planet.

We can only hope to awaken you to your own power before you destroy all life. You are the decision-makers. Each thought you hold, each core-belief you cling to WILL TAKE FORM.

Look closely at what you believe. Often it is that one thing that you say, "Ah, yes, I understand, **but** this is true." What is true? That the government is made up of evil men? Visit your local courthouse, your city hall, your state offices, your governmental buildings. You will find people just like yourself, talking about the latest TV show, their love affairs and their financial difficulties.

Look behind your beliefs. Look behind your fears. YOU are the answer to World Peace today and forever.

10. As we look at the current scenario of upheaval, it is obvious that all structures that do not serve the needs of humanity and the planet are being disrupted and destroyed. They are falling by their own weight. The ground is being furrowed, and the seeds for a new reality have been sown.

What will grow? The probabilities for the human race, planet earth, the solar system and galaxy are infinite, just as your personal probabilities are infinite.

The train of thought we have introduced in a nutshell is

as follows: Your planet is traveling through an acceleration beam, which will result in a birthing of Global Consciousness, followed by a meeting with other planetary representatives who have gone through similar circumstances.

The probable outcome of those events would result in a blossoming of creativity and expansion of consciousness never before imagined upon this Plane.

There would be a reconsideration of all structures and the establishment of organically designed teams to heal the planet and all areas of life.

Councils of experts in every field cooperating on a community, state, national and planetary level would be organized to address the needs of the environment, animal welfare, health, eduction, housing, agriculture, transportation, business, governmental structures, finance, distribution, etc.

All new structures would be organized to enhance an integration of all areas of life. Cosmic consultants would offer advice and counsel with the implicit understanding that human beings are the caretakers, and are thus responsible for healing themselves and the Planet Earth.

It is upon you and your friends. We are here to be called upon. You are the decision-makers.

You may choose chaos and confusion and continue the drama of victim and aggressor into extinction.

Or you may choose love, joy, peace, harmony, nurturing, caring, partnership and continue the evolutionary experience of the species.

Chapter 7

Julian

Channeled by June Burke

June Burke worked in earlier years as an artist, illustrator and sculptor at the Museum of Science and Industry at Rockefeller Center in New York City. She is a wife, mother and grandmother, and for the last 29 years has been a deep, or full trance, medium. Her mediumship came following a near-death experience.

Man has, because of his attachment to time and the measurement of it in linear form, struggled to understand the creation. He constantly tries to put creation into his context rather than to seek to understand it as nebulous energy. Respecting the linear understanding by which mankind functions, I will try to clarify the creation theory for you.

Creation was (and is) energy in movement. All that is, or can be, was. The so-called void was non-directed energy. It was empty of conceived movement. It was the pulsating energy of pure potential. The yet to be. By the very nature of that potential the energy moved upon itself, creating movement through expansion and contraction. It would continue to do so for thousands of years.

Let us use a mundane example: a pint of cream, sealed and set aside. As time passes, by the nature of its own potential, it moves upon itself and alters its energy. Expansion and contraction begins and cellular potential alters. That energy can become volatile and explosive.

The quality of the original energy is changed and becomes a new component of its ultimate potential. Limited thinking says it is cream – period. Creative evolution says it is cream only in one of its potential forms.

So, too, did creation become volatile and explosive. Its vibration increased and began to form a rhythm within which it vibrated.

After building up over thousands more years it finally exploded, casting off pulsating parts of itself. It is at this point that the big bang theory came into being. The so called "Big Bang" was a natural part of the whole of creation. Creation is movement in evolution.

These rhythmic, vibrating parts each carried with them the identity, through movement, of that from which they came. They would become, through their own evolutionary process, universes in their own right.

All creation carries in it the replica of that origin energy. In essence, through your own cellular movement, you are made in the image of creation. The stamp of that original source energy and its rhythm and movement is repeated in all things.

Within the pattern of rhythm and movement the qualities of energy began to separate, alter and move upon themselves according to their altered energy. Each quality contained within it the rhythm of the universe whose structure it vibrated under.

These alterings brought forth the separation into the elements. Each element held within it the origin pattern of continuance through movement and separation. Each would continue to grow and evolve in its own right.

They would come to be recognized as air, fire, water and earth, having the qualities of movement and space, expansion, contraction and solidification. From them all else would form. The qualities of each is needed for formation.

It would be over forty thousand years before the cell of mankind would begin the move upon itself and become the essence form of what would later solidify, densify and become homo sapiens.

The universe, carrying within it the order and pattern of the origin energy, was beginning to evolve. It was learning to express through the intuitive direction from that pattern. That the pattern contained an order and an inner direction became clear.

There was a division within the energies and a clearly

defined sense of purpose in relationship to the evolution of that which had been created.

Those things of nature and space would remain non-personal in their rhythm and vibrations. They would be responsible for the natural changes needed for the evolution of and perpetuem of the universe and all within it. They would become the governing energy of the universe, bring necessary change to it about every three thousand years.

(See Illustration 1, page 110)

As mankind continued to evolve and grow, he began to identify more fully with himself. He took the inner pattern into a personalized expression.

The natural forces used instinct and intuitive understanding to function, while man developed a thinking, mental pattern of expression. Functioning under universal instinct, man would, through his more personalized energies, develop a will and a desire to express mentally. His more personal attitude would bring him into the evolutionary spiral of a two-thousand-six-hundred year rhythm.

These rhythms are the pulsation of the creative potential, the breathing in and breathing out which sustains energy and permits movement. Everything within that rhythm has a vibration which is its individual identity to the universe.

It is through the interaction of these energies individually and collectively that evolution occurs. Man's individual spiral interacts with and becomes mankind's collective spiral which affects the movement of the universe's governing spiral. They are spirals, one within the other, with each affecting the other. It is at this point that creation, as man understands it through theology, begins. The seven days of creation as taught biblically do not consist of seven twenty-four hour periods. Each day was roughly 1500 years in time.

Fifteen hundred years in which the evolutionary process would repeat and renew itself again and again. Each renewal moved that evolution forward and changed the energies once again. Each "day" developed a specific quality for the universe.

(See Illustration 2, page 111)

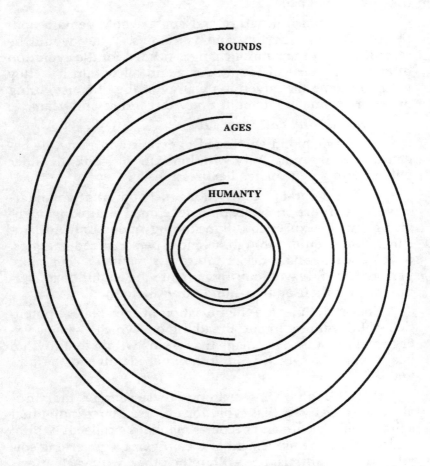

Man Gestates Within the Universal Womb.
The Ages Feed His Evolution.
The Rounds Cleanse and Build His Space.

Illustration 1.

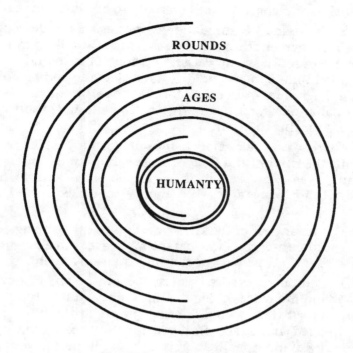

DAYS & ROUNDS

1. **MOVEMENT** - Vibration
2. **BREATH** - Action
3. **SPIRIT** - Intuition
4. **THOUGHT** - Mind
5. **COMMUNICATION** - Space
6. **FORM** - Physical
7. **FLOW** - Adjustment

Illustration 2

The energy now began to follow a formed, directed pattern. The void, through its own natural movement of expansion and contraction, separated to become the species.

Each energy became its own species. Each developed its own atunement through the senses first and then through mental action. The mind became the tool for mankind which permitted him to focus and direct his own and source potential energies. He could think, form an idea, tap the universal potential and bring it forth. Again, it would take thousands of years for this to occur.

There was a mathematical formula forming which would become the rhythm and flow of the creation for all time. This formula was expressed in the seasons. Each quarter in a cycle would bring a specific energy to be expressed and used.

The balancing of darkness and light at the spring equinox would permit the same balancing to occur in all creation. It would encourage new beginnings and movement.

The summer solstice's energy would be one of nurturing and maintenance of that begun. Once again, through the fall equinox, balance would permit the reward of those energies directed and used. In the winter solstice would come the energy of inner realization which would permit preparation for the next spring's new launching. Even man would be as a seed, filled with the potential to become what he was meant to become. The universal energies in their cycles would encourage man to move and develop them.

Each universe, and at the present time there are seven of them, starts as a closed force in order to direct its energy to the evolution of itself and all it contains. As full awareness is developed those universes will begin to slowly open to each other. This will take thousands and thousands of years.

To understand the universe's relationship to you is important. Recognizing that your energies are related assists you in using them more fully. One thing to accept is that the movement is a forward one. If you become too enamored of that which was, so that you do not live that which is, you slow yourself down.

You are now living in the age called Aquarius. It is the age of brotherhood. Nineteen-hundred and ninety-one is the fifteenth year of the two-thousand-six-hundred year span. It is now that man evolves away from hatred and accepts peace. This age is governed by nature and the polarities.

Man will again recognize his relationship to nature and will bring inner balance to himself and his universe. He must bring balance between work and play, activity and rest. It is in this point in time that there must be brought about acceptance and new perspective.

These are the keys to the energies used now. Accept where you are in order to evaluate it and understand it. Only then can you change it. Change is brought about by new perspective. Looking at something differently can change how you handle it and how you are affected by it.

Awareness of balance is paramount in this point in time. Man must realize that his body and mind are integral parts of his spirit. It is important that his temple (body) be cared for, for this is the indwelling place of the soul. The necessity of balanced eating patterns becomes very important in this high-frequency energy.

This means each individual striking the balance that is right for his energy. Extremes are not the answer. There are certain foods that are important to the body and should be included in the eating pattern. Onion, celery, cabbage, broccoli, parsnips and potatoes are foods that assist in the maintenance of muscle and tissue tone. The key, even in nutrition, is balance. There is no better or only way that is right. Choose the pattern that fits your energy. Some energies need meat, others do not.

Each age seals off certain bacteria when it comes in, and opens others due to the frequency change. Many people will now find themselves being less affected by allergies that have long bothered them.

The decade of the nineties is the decade of transition energy. It is the release of the past and the acceptance of the future. It is a very powerful point in time. It is the power of a three-thousand year round, a new two-thousand-six-hundred year age and a new decade all at once.

Mankind is in this decade moving to a fuller comprehension of the light body from which he came. He will again have the opportunity to touch that frequency for the first time since the beginning. He will experience what light means and begin the evolutionary process it permits.

In 1990 and 1991, major changes occurred. These may seem negative for they deal with the breaking up of old spaces, habits and patterns. While this releases man to his greater potential, the fact that this potential is not clearly defined may make him feel uneasy.

Man himself is experiencing the changes in vibration that the universe is experiencing. Now is the time when man truly begins to release that which no longer serves him and moves toward his full potential.

When you understand that all things contain the same pattern or formula, brought forth from that original energy source, you begin to understand that physical man is affected by the changes within the universe brought about by those higher non-personal energies which direct the movement of that universe.

The planetary energies are each responsible for specific energy interactions at specific times in their evolutionary rounds. These energies touch the inner pattern in man and help him bring about the necessary changes he is meant to experience. It helps him get out of his rut.

At this point in time man himself is vibrating at the highest rate he has ever vibrated at because his universe is. This higher frequency changes not only his viewpoint, but also his own physical reactions. In this decade man can take stronger control of his physical will by understanding the very oneness of all things.

When an age changes, the old energy is gradually sealed and the new potentials are opened. This alters the affect of the power of disease and brings greater ability to understand it and overcome it.

Energy is an inherent power which alters and changes by natural (intuitive) or mental direction. Vibration alters the energy level. All things in creation are energy in motion. The vibration creates the degree of the force of its expression.

Physical man inherits his tendencies from two sources. His own innate memory of that original power source, which permits him to bring forth from that energy, and his physical genes which are the by-product of the male and female genes of the parents. **The most powerful inheritance is the origin-source energy.**

This, used correctly, can overcome any idiosyncrasy of genetic influence. The evolution of this point in time permits man to recognize this fact and begin to understand its use. During the previous age, he sought external guidance.

In this age he turns inward to that power which in turn empowers him. Altering this energy affects man mentally, emotionally, physically and spiritually.

Mind is the tool which permits man to direct energy.

At this point in time man is experiencing multiple energy changes. Everything within him responds to these vibratory escalations.

Many people may feel uneasy, because the constant changes make them feel unsure of who they are. These changes are pushed by the universe, whose job it is to present them in order that man may use them to move forward.

Understand that the rate of vibration of the energy alters man's inner universe creating cellular change and the altering and strengthening of mental capacity. The mind is the tool used to expand or decrease the body's action.

One can literally think himself into illness or to wholeness. The thought increases or decreases the energy of the cell, thus altering it and creating change. Inside man the creation aspect occurs. He casts off and rebuilds constantly.

Health is literally a product of balance. It is mental, physical and spiritual. The mind must be stimulated, the body nurtured and the spirit enlightened.

If a person looks on everything in life as an imposition, he will find life very trying.

His mental attitude will color everything else. Eventually he will create the same attitude within his physical body because the body is the only place he has in which to manifest his thoughts.

The degree to which you permit anything to affect you will equal the degree of power it has over your physical being. To be a truly healthy being, I suggest the practice of these things:

1. Use a healing affirmation to start your day.

2. Each day practice mental interaction with others. Let yourself move to thoughts not centered on you.

3. Feed the physical self with balance and moderation. Be sure your diet includes greens and roughage. Create an inner space of peace when you eat!

4. Exercise in some form. Walking is a full body exercise and is excellent. Housework can also be used as an exercise. Use exercises that use your joints. Again, moderation is preferred over erratic overparticipation. Breathe deeply to oxygenate the mind.

5. Spend at least fifteen to twenty minutes a day in silence. Meditate or sit quietly with yourself, letting the mind still. Permit the sensory aspects of the self to be felt.

6. Each day, practice the art of letting go. Take an incident, think about it, thank it for its lessons, bless it, wish it well and release it. Letting go of negative attitudes daily saves a lot of built-up misery from things held on to and amplified by constant thought of them.

7. Smile, and better yet, permit yourself to laugh daily. Life has many happy moments. Permit yourself to enjoy them. A sunny day or a bird drinking from a puddle bath both have the power to lift your spirits and free you emotionally if you permit them to.

8. Each day, try seeing things through "somebody else's glasses" for a little while. It will get you out of yourself and broaden your ability to understand others.

9. Incidents in life are like embers from a fire. How much you fan them makes them become more fierce or permits them to cool and die. Practice the art of sorting which is to be which, daily.

10. Lastly, touch yourself! Thank your body, mind and spirit for helping you to be emotionally sound. Don't use ill health as a cop-out! Let yourself love you enough to be willing to be honest with yourself.

Affirmations for Change

1. *I am an infinite spirit in physical form.*
   I am guided daily from infinite mind.
   I am movement in evolution and free to change.
   I am my power, my projection and my manifestation.

2. *I accept that wholeness is mine.*
   I permit it to permeate my entire being.
   Mind, body and spirit – I am whole.

3. *There is inner guidance leading me now.*
   I accept it and am freed from negativity.
   I joyously release my full potential to my
   higher self and I achieve.

4. *All that I need or desire becomes mine, through*
   correct thought and action.
   I am the master of all that I am.
   I am fulfilled by this realization.

5. *I release all preconceived ideas about my health.*
   I accept that change can and will occur.
   Each day shows evidence that this is so.

One of the greatest problems in health areas is fear. Fear of failing, fear of success, fear of making a mistake. Mistakes are part of evolution, too. Learn from them and use them as a stepping stone to something else. Whatever happened, happened. You can't change that, but you can change the degree of power that it has over you. Learn from it and move on.

Practice the art of handling what you can handle right now. Break down the overwhelming whole into smaller parts. Then work on one part at a time.

Worrying about the "whole thing" hinders the ability to solve it. When any part is solved it alters the outcome of the whole. Worry and stress break down the "whole" aspect of your health. When you work with it, facet by facet, you are controlling it, rather than letting it control you.

Remember that what you think becomes your reality. Direct the thoughts to positive progressive things. Use mental imagery to bring change. Affirm the power of you in a changing universe.

Chapter 8

NOVA 8

Channeled by Norman

Vortexes, simply put, are spiralling streams of energy that contain within them the Light patterns (codes) which define creation. When Light is first cast forth from the Source it interacts with itself, dividing into various rays or properties as if it were passed through a prism. Specific properties are then redirected based on their ability to contribute to the manifestation of a desired experience.

Manifestation occurs as soon as the properties or rays of Light are projected (focused) by way of vortexes and made to intersect with one another forming a holographic image.

Be it a brilliant star, the miracle of the human body, or a gently rolling stream, everything is created by Light.

In order for a created image to have a life span, the Light projections must remain constant in all respects. When the projection is altered, so is the creation, and subsequently the experience. And like television, as long as there's an energy supply, an image will remain.

When it is time to change the station and move on to another experience, the Light projections can be altered in several different ways, either individually or collectively.

The major tools for change include:

1. Realigning one or more of the vortexes, which may affect the relative location of the image as well as its design;

2. Adjusting the vibratory frequency of the patterns by stepping down or amplifying the Light projections (adding or subtracting the number of filters, so to speak), which adjusts

the density of the form; and/or

3. Varying the Light values/rays within the vortexes by increasing or decreasing certain properties and/or their intensities. This influences the creative expression, as a painter would do with a paintbrush.

The origin of all creation, whether it be the human structure with its chakras or a planet with its "sacred sites,"* can be traced through its vortexes. Planet Earth resulted from the convergence of 12 + 1 primary vortexes which represented all patterns of creation ever experienced by the many and one Universe.

Each vortex, containing a specific ray of Light with its full spectrum of expression, was directed by the Creators and guided through specific star systems until it intersected with other vortexes at an agreed-upon point in time and space.

When this took place, an identifiable field of energy (a Light pattern or "planetary grid") was established, taking the form of what is now recognized as a paradise planet.

As seen by the Creators, the vortexes appear as great arcs of multicolored Light corkscrewing back and forth along interstellar pathways (cosmic highways, so to speak), and converging in a ball of rainbow essence before returning to their Source.

To experience the vortexes allow your Self to be drawn to a location that you naturally prefer. These "natural attractions" occur because the Light properties are also a part of the human encodement.

Therefore, each soul has a corresponding relationship with a specific ray and vortex. Those who are in harmony with the Light patterns will be magnetized to the vortex which matches their personal encoding.

To be in harmony is to be in step with one's natural order of evolution and synchronized with the flow of Universal events. By exemplifying only Love, being free of fear and doubt, and open to change and acceptance of others, you will greatly enhance this process.

––––––––

*The sacred sites are those areas where the vortexes intersect with the surface of the planet. The locations of the 12+1 primary vortexes are encoded in Chapter 2 of the Book of Numbers within the Old Testament.

For those interested in information relating to one's personal relationship with the Light patterns (the templates defining sound, color and numerical sequence/mathematics manifested within the DNA matrix of the human vessel), it can be accessed by way of meditation, contemplation, or other inner personal methods.

These "codes" reveal not only the blueprint for one's role within the planetary program, but also the pathway for soul evolution beyond the third dimension.

Many individuals are now locating their "natural" homes on the planet as we enter this final period of transition. Such periods occur when an energy configuration of a particular existence passes and a new image takes its place (likened to an ice cube melting into a pool of water).

The vibratory frequencies of Earth's elements are now being raised, reducing the density/limitations of the matter and expanding states of consciousness (awareness of one's existence and environment) of the souls embodying it.

All third dimensional energy patterns (whether physical manifestations or thoughts held within the mental, emotional, and astral bodies) are now being stimulated to support the soul's journey through the many dimensions of the Universe.

The thirteenth vortex, identified as "+1," holds a special role in Earth's period of transition. It is sometimes referred to as the energy "capstone," for not only does it contain all encodings of past and present planetary cycles, it also holds the activation codes that initiate the final sequence of events for the ascension of the planet into the fourth dimension and beyond.

It is here that a new Light pattern is being projected that provides for the transformation of all that exists within our present reality.

This 13th Light pattern is equivalent to a grand tuning fork that resonates the vibratory frequencies represented in the fourth dimension so that all third dimensional creations can tune to the next octave of existence.

Entities who visit this sacred region, as well as the other vortex sites, will be affected in some way by the higher frequency Light projections. If not in harmony, they may feel somewhat 'out of sync,' to say the least. However, once attuned to the energies, they will begin to experience a greater sense of Christ consciousness as they become the tuning forks for others.

Jesus exemplified Christ consciousness because he was in tune with this vibration. The healing that took place in his presence resulted from individual contact with these more refined energy patterns. In order to be a similar conduit for channeling these energies and for raising the frequency of one's own essence, it is necessary to remain clear and balanced in all respects – physically, emotionally, mentally and spiritually.

The history of Earth's vortexes began at the moment the thought of such a planet was originated. That set off all the necessary forces to separate, project, direct and intersect the Light properties desired for the planetary pattern.

Since it was agreed that all aspects of previous creation would be incorporated into this pattern, each of the twelve Universes (the Universes of the Universes) supplied a ray of Light that contained all elements of its being.

When all radiations of these Universes were 'seeded' (focused) into the far reaches of the Milky Way Galaxy, the energy forces, which eventually gave birth to the planet's physical manifestation, began to evolve.

At this point in Earth's brief history, the vortexes were in perfect alignment with Universal Law. The flow of Light and Love was abundant and all of the planetary components were evolving naturally.

Then, at a predetermined time, the primary vortexes were intentionally altered by the Creators, so that Earth could be freed from strict adherence to its original blueprint.

In the process, it was isolated from the rest of Creation and left to evolve without the assistance of the higher frequency energies that are normally available.

The reasons for this action were twofold:

1. So that souls could experience "free will" completely independent of the influences of the One Mind (the collective consciousness of "All That Is").

2. So that others within the Universe would be less apt to interfere with the experiment. Thus, the stage was set to experience the illusion of being separated consciously from the Source.

Since vortexes are the life support systems of creation, they provide the basic energy units for the planet's survival. When they were realigned they provided only minimum requirements for planetary evolution. In effect, they became dormant, waiting to receive the higher frequencies necessary to facilitate a subsequent planetary program.

The changes to the vortexes also impacted certain entities outside of the immediate Earth realm. Although all who were not directly participating in this experiment were notified that they should remain outside the region of influence, a few souls did not heed the warnings.

Following their own will, these souls entered the forbidden area and soon found themselves cut off from the higher energies to which they were accustomed. As a result, they slowly began to lose consciousness. The memory of who they were became distorted. The divine characteristic of Love was forgotten and the freedom associated with knowing the truth was lost.

In hopes of gaining back their freedom, the misplaced souls proceeded to mastermind control of Earth and her inhabitants. As an example, they were able to convince humans to look externally for a god who actually resides within.

In this way, the embodied souls became subservient to self-proclaimed gods who have been portrayed as wrathful, jealous and judgmental.

These 'lesser gods' are so adept in projecting thought patterns into the planetary consciousness that most souls have remained in the darkness of ignorance during their entire sojourn on Earth – blindly obedient to religions and other institutions whose purpose is to control the masses.

When the primary vortexes were altered, the road maps between planets, star systems and Universes had to be redrawn. Thus it was not long before the Earth-based souls found themselves completely disoriented relative to the signposts – the stars. Some entities became so confused that they retreated to the inner Earth regions, where many remain today. They are joined by others who have moved within to seek refuge from thought forms of the 'lesser gods' which were grossly afflicting the surface plane.

It is important to appreciate that all of what has taken place on Earth, regardless of how it is judged, has provided important elements to this most ambitious experiment.

All activities, whether originally planned or the outbreak of circumstance, have fulfilled a purpose. As we now regain the understanding of Self and our role within the greater plan, we will be able to accept this truth.

Recently, the primary vortexes were brought back into harmony with the natural order of the Universe. This was orchestrated by the Creators in cooperation with their Earth-based representatives.

As of mid-year 1989, all sites were reactivated as a critical mass of Earth energy/consciousness attuned to the higher frequency Light projections. Thus a harmonizing rhythm has been imposed, and more orderliness has entered the system.

A vast human network is now firmly in place (aided by other kingdoms including both the elemental and angelic), that is in harmony with the higher frequency projections.

Those within this network are at one with the Christ vibration and thereby are beginning to receive the fourth-dimensional experience in this plane of existence. The Christ has returned as a collective Messiah of human consciousness!

With this phase of the planetary program complete, Earth with all of its life forms has taken a major step toward an expanded state of consciousness.

Soon it will be able to overcome the density/limitations associated with our present existence, anchored in thoughts and actions emanating from fear, doubt, judgment, jealousy, the desire to control the free will of others, and so on.

These old patterns will become more evident as they interact with other 'non-harmonious' energies which have been dispelled recently from the higher realms (that is, 'the lesser gods').

All that is 'non-harmonious' will remain in the third dimension until it is in harmony with the higher frequencies, or is translated when Earth ascends.

This most likely will create more chaos and confusion in those who are not adapting to the changes.

As part of the activation process, the vortexes were 'fine-tuned' to accommodate the changes which occurred throughout all of creation over the course of this planetary program.

Earth is now in alignment with the key interdimensional doorways corresponding to Universal time/space/event sequences (including activities within parallel time zones).

These doorways are also known as portals or stargates. They provide safe, orderly passage throughout the many and one Universe.

The portals on the surface plane and in the inner Earth region, as well as the astral realms, are now positioned to allow unrestricted movement of souls. This represents a major provision for the *first call* to souls who have evolved beyond the third dimension Earth experience.

The doorways are accessible to those who have made their departure preparations, as evidenced by their evolvement beyond third dimensional patterns and their willingness to take responsibility for entering into the next octave of existence. Key to this preparation is the desire to *let go* of the human drama while embracing unlimited thinking.

A *second call* shall be made prior to the release of the last major energy forces necessary to complete the planetary balancing and cleansing. This next summons will support those souls who do not desire to experience that which shall ensue.

The *third and final call* shall come forth prior to the transformation of third dimension Earth, and will respond to entities whose options will be limited severely by the conditions prevalent in the final days.

For those who do not resonate with these signals sent forth by the One Mind there are provisions for the relocation of souls (with or without physical vessels) to other planetary realms of similar circumstance where the evolutionary process can be carried out according to the individual's will.

These calls, in response to the changes that are taking place on Earth and beyond, should be taken quite seriously. The higher frequency energies are affecting all of Earth's creation, including embodied souls, without exception. Here are some reasons why:

1. The Light is shining ever so brightly on the truth of one's presence in the Universal order. Once a person accepts that he or she is an integral part of a greater plan, then it will be clear why it is so important to be in harmony with what is taking place. The old patterns must be released (now) to make way for the changes.

If this happens, the collective consciousness of the planet can expand and all will be positioned to move on to experience other realms. If there is resistance to the change, then it will be only through great ordeal that the purposes of the higher frequencies will be realized.

2. The vortexes are providing greater life support for the planet as pure energies pour forth from the Source. When Earth fully embraces these higher energies, she can breathe new life into all her aspects, thereby releasing the limitations or densities previously accepted. All shall be made new!

3. The vortexes can now transport beings of higher frequencies to Earth without the previous restrictions. This is most significant as there are many who have come to this far region of the Universe to assist in the personal and planetary ascension process.

But because these galactic emissaries have difficulty withstanding dense thought forms, Earthlings are being asked to prepare for their arrival by releasing all non-harmonious thought forms. Projecting Light and love into everything and everyone is an absolute requirement.

It is interesting that people from all over the earth are being drawn to these vortexes and are establishing communities to utilize the energies to create new, loving and Light environments. These settlements are being called Communities of Light.

Communities of Light are environments where those who participate have a common interest in exploring the truth of their being with a primary desire to move consciously beyond the limited thinking of the third dimensional realm.

In other words, these living environments are the meeting grounds for taking full responsibility for the changes as both Creator and created.

The Communities of Light take on many forms, depending on the needs and desires of the participants. Essentially, they are a response to going within and acknowledging what works and what does not. Once this has been clearly established, the physical manifestation arises out of the love and devotion to make it happen.

If you love something enough (this includes your dreams and visions), this will respond back according to your greatest desires. If you would love to be in an environment which supports your spiritual growth and creativity, then it will be so.

If you love to love others, you will create an environment which provides you such an opportunity. If you love to be loved, this is equally true.

If your love is to create heaven on Earth, allow yourself to manifest this reality, for if this is your true love, then it must happen. Let go your doubts and fears, for the love of which is spoken is unconditional – it has no polarity or opposing force.

Communities of Light can be considered the islands which, when united, form a sea of tranquility that exists outside of time. They represent the foundation stones upon which a smooth transition into a higher vibrational reality can be made. They are the result of choices made by souls and groups of souls who acknowledge the contribution that love has in lighting the way.

The intentional communities are not just living environments which occur in the remote woods or high on the desert plains. They start in the environment where you are right now. It is just a matter of loving yourself and all that comprises your life including all thoughts and actions.

This love for "All That Is" eventually may pull you into another more preferred environment, but it is essential to the process that you change your attitude right now. If you cannot express the love that is within, it will not matter where you are externally. Once you have accepted the love that allows you to manifest your self-identity, then you can expand that awareness to embrace your entire reality – the ONE.

The islands become the continent that becomes the Earth that becomes "All That Is" – the one then becomes the One!

Perhaps this sounds a little too easy after all the struggles you have faced during the experience of separation. You will never know until you try. Try loving yourself in the way that you would like *another* to love you. Then love the *other* like you want to be loved.

Maybe, just maybe, you will get so entangled in this love that you will not have time to replay the past, or worry about the future.

If you get caught up in this love for yourself and for **"All That Is,"** you will realize wisdom and joy – for what else would love provide?

In closing, it is worth remembering that we have all participated on Earth's third dimensional platform to gain an understanding of what it would be like to be separated consciously from the One Mind/Source/God/I Am that I AM — or whatever you use to describe the **"All That Is."**

We have survived our self-imposed experience, and in the process have explored the many facets of independent will. It is now time to take the wisdom which we have acquired and move back into harmony with the truth of **"All That Is."**

We are beings of Light and citizens of the Universe, and the way home is through the vortexes of our consciousness.

Chapter 9

One Drop of the Cosmic Christ

Channeled by Tuieta

(To the reader: You will note certain "unusual" phrases and spelling of words in the following text. This is the way they were impressed upon my conscious mind by the beloved one known to me as One Drop of the Cosmic Christ. Tuieta)

In the Light of the Source, I Am. Peace unto all ones. I speak as One Drop of the Cosmic Christ. I am the consciousness beyond the separateness, the consciousness of the Oneness coming forth to unite all in love, Divine Essence in self and Divine Essence in all others. I speak from the knowing of the Christ, that which is beyond the comprehension of mortal man. Yet, I bring to man an understanding so he might stand within that which I Am to proclaim of his own divinity. I have not face or form but I say I am the face and form of all, even to that which lies unborn within the womb of creation awaiting its expression, its actualization.

The Law of Attraction within the parameters of duality attempts balance out of unbalance. This is illustrated most admirably in the unit which is know as man – the being of Earth who carries a consciousness of Divine Connection.

Even in the relationship, the coming together of the male and female to produce child, it is the seeking of balance within the immediate environs to allow for a stability of experience or opportunity for the actualization of the Divine Essence.

It represents the search for the acceptance which can

only be realized as the individuals accept themselves and the Essence which they are.

Man does not, say deny, the completeness of himself because through life times of indoctrination he accepts the half of himself that is the male or female. He envisions a relationship with the opposite sex bringing a balance to his unbalance. The sexual action is seen as the ultimate expression of coming and melding into oneness. This is an external search for an internal process.

The sexual act, the act of procreation, has been touted, revered and idolized as the ultimate of individual expression. Indeed, the Judeo-Christian community of Earth touts the physical attributes of both the male and female for gain of monies and goods. The search for the perfection of the individual and the actualization of Divine Essence continues in man's progression to his Source, realization.

The procreative aspects of a relationship are a triune experience of the father-mother-child, the father-mother within the dimensional parameters and the "child" from realms beyond the dimension. As in the dimensional creation, the Divine thought enters to cause displacement, random movement, then attraction and bonding.

This same process is repeated as the egg and sperm unite to bring about a new being capable of housing the Divine Essence of another. At the exact moment when the attraction and bonding cycle begins the influence of the incoming one is realized. This begins by the selection of the sex of the form best suited to allow for the greatest opportunity of experience, to allow the Christ self to actualize within the dimension of duality.

The incoming one arranges the attraction pattern within the egg or ovum to attract the appropriate chromosome to its mate to be either male or female. From that point until the release at the birthing process the pattern of formation is orchestrated by the one waiting to enter.

The host parent, the mother, provides the tool or laboratory for the process. Even how she does this is overshadowed by the one awaiting the form. (This "miracle" occurs at the level which is yet to be understood or explained by your scientists.) The influence of guidance continues until the soul no longer needs the vehicle and releases it to return to the components of the dimension, thus freeing the soul for multidimensional expression.

How is this done? As the incomplete sets of chromosomes come together to begin a new life cycle, the "soul," the Divine Essence, knowing of its previous experiences arranges the chromosomal pattern in a way best suited to bring about the optimum opportunities for the expression of highest order for the Divine Essence.

This can be likened to programing a computer. As you are aware, with a computer you can only receive specific actions within a program because the capability of the computer with its program is limited to the program. There are times when the program holds more information than the operator knows.

Then, "quite by accident," the operator stumbles on a part of the program which had previously been unavailable. The operator then begins an exploration of that "new found" program portion and uses it with the established or known portion. Is not our life cycle such as this?

The Divine Essence programs its desires/needs into the DNA pattern of the cell. Chromosomes arrange to comply with that desired need. You see this as eye color, height, weight, intelligence and much more. You see the result of this influence or programming as the individual. The soul's eye sees the vehicle for divine expression.

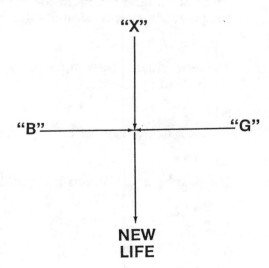

Figure 1

STEP 1.

Soul "B" + Soul "G" + Soul "X" = agreement.

STEP 2.

Soul "B" enters Life cycle.

Refer to Figure 1 on page 131.

STEP 3.

Soul "G" enters Life cycle.

STEP 4.

Soul "B" + Soul "G" come together because of
attraction of genetic commitment.

STEP 5.

Soul "X" waits for act of soul "B" and soul "G".

STEP 6.

Pattern established by act *(Figure 1, p. 131)*.

STEP 7.

"X" projects energy at time of conception to
program new vehicle, life form.

STEP 8.

DNA sets cellular reproduction into operation
carrying the instructions from soul to each cell to
bring about and maintain the vehicle best suited
for the divine expression for this experience.

STEP 9.

The soul enters the completed form, initiating
the birthing process.

STEP 10.

Birthing or delivery of the new form.

STEP 11.

The first breath of life or independent act of new life.

STEP 12.

A cycle begins.

This is the conceptual process of form creation. This is the process used to allow for the experience of your dimension. Without the influence of the third party or the soul of the incoming one, there is no expression of the divine.

Scientists in your laboratories have reproduced cellular division but there is the limitation without the influence bringing about a triune energy. The process of external or outside the female fertilization which represents the triune flow can be used to actualize a previous agreement of the three souls.

However, in man's desire for experimentation and scientific study he is denying the contribution of the incoming agent in the total process. The desire for pleasure, immortality and acceptance by the collective has lead man into routes of study which are unbeneficial for him. The desire to produce a super being or race is a driving force behind the genetic engineering mode.

The super being is the one who is the actualization of the Christ Consciousness within the Earth plane. This cannot be accomplished in laboratories or genetic experiments.

But let us continue with the cycle of a new life – a new opportunity for divine expression. As you who have an individual soul are deities, you are desiring to express your deity through the process of experience. These experiences for divine expression are not limited to the earth plane but are available cosmically. *(See Figure 2, p. 134)*

The experience of the earth plane, because its density brings about the dimension of duality, is a unique one. In your thoughts of the educational process, the earth experience offers an accelerated opportunity of experiences to express the God Consciousness within you.

There is, however, one agreement one makes when they enter the accelerated program. One must stay in the program until they have achieved a balance of experiences and have expressed their deity in the cumulative experience.

The DNA is represented to earth-man as a unit of attracting capabilities within the nucleus of the cell. It seems to hold an intelligence in programming. It can open itself to allow part of itself to go forth as the RNA in the total process of cell production and reproduction. The DNA now appears to hold the link to the origin of the creative process. The

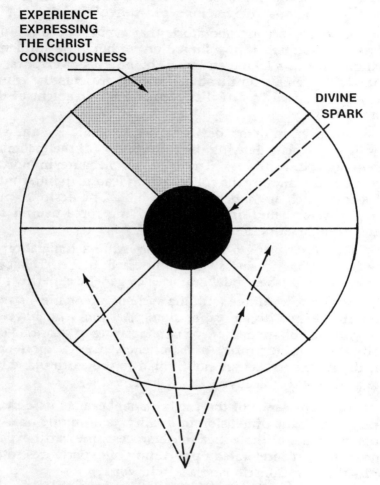

EXPERIENCE
EXPRESSING
THE CHRIST
CONSCIOUSNESS

DIVINE
SPARK

INDIVIDUAL LIFETIMES/FACETS OF EXPER-
IENCES IN WHICH THE CONSCIOUSNESS HAS
NOT BEEN EXPRESSED. AN UNBALANCE WHICH
GENERATES CONTINUED EXPERIENCE POTEN-
TIAL OF CHRIST ACTUALIZATION.

Figure 2

genes contained in the chromosomes of the male and female come together to make a complete unit of two sets of incomplete units.

The DNA of these cells is seeking balance for expression out of the unbalance of their waiting existence. Within the DNA factor of the cell lies a great mystery which Earth has yet to explore. To date, this exploration has been of the procreative level.

The DNA has two facets. That which is known by scientists which is the dominant and that which is not, which might be called the latent or unexpressed. It is of the latent and existing energy vibrations we shall explore.

The latent facet is the all-knowing which is not confined to or limited by the parameters of your dimension. It is the facet which, when allowed to express is the divine representative of the God Force. Each cell of your being has this knowing, is waiting to express the God Essence you are.

You, within the parameters of your dimension operate or function within a specific vibration of energy. This specific vibration holds density of everything within it so all might be in a harmonious pattern. Even within your mental process you can demonstrate an alteration of density as the vibration is altered. This alteration in vibration can be experienced by you in multiple ways.

Initially the most frequent experience is one of reaction. This is first at the cellular level of the body and then is felt generally throughout. One feels uneasy, irritable, undefined. There is a restlessness whose origin cannot be pinpointed. Reaction becomes paramount in the individual's life. This in some instances is taken to the point of the very survival of the individual. The focus on self, its needs, its desires, become the driving force. All others, all relationships are seen as opportunities to serve self.

Some would define this individual as extremely self-centered, even quite selfish. This is a stage in which the ego, recognizing the initial alteration of the relationship of the dominant and latent facets of the life defining factors, is expressing the change in energy balance between the two. That which was accepted as being, now is no longer accepted. Energy vibration alteration is being experienced internally, demonstrating the interconnectedness of everything.

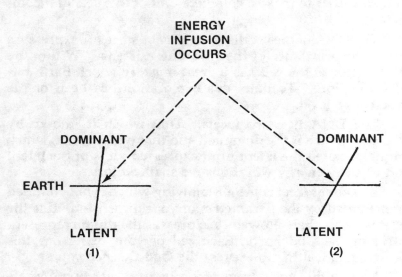

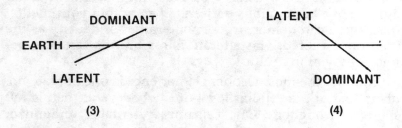

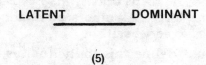

Figure 3

(Note: As you observe items 1-5 in Figure 3, the individual is accepting of the altered energy vibration, thus experiencing a balancing of the dominant and latent facets within self.)

All vibrational patterns of energy are cyclical with one cycle building upon the previous. As a result the balancing of the dominant and latent facets of the DNA are in direct relation to the vibrational pattern.

Even as you have been schooled in your unworthiness and the "fall from grace," know these are erroneous teachings. Their origin served a ministry seeking its own preservation and reason for being.

The total you present today is a result of all you have expressed in your dimension. You could be no less or no more because you were not at a point you could respond to the vibrational pattern if it had been present.

The slower the vibration the greater is the dominant facet of the DNA and the more all of the activities related to life are focused on the density of the dimension.

Those within the dimension holding Earth are within the dimensional parameters to present opportunity to experience the implementation of Divine Will within those parameters.

As each facet of the Godhead/Central Source has opportunity so it is there is the dimension or space defined for the experience. With the opportunity and the successful expression of the facet of the source then the parameters thin allowing the integration with all which has, and ever will be experienced.

How better can you express Divine Will than to be in a state of duality? This state can be represented as a straight line with opposites at either end.

"X" <_____> the total opposite of "X "

good <_____> bad

This distinct limitation allows you to choose constantly. The choice in the majority of instances is toward the dominant facet of your DNA. As the vibrational pattern of the energy about your planet is altered so it is there is an alteration in your choosing. There sets up a struggle within the individual at the cellular level. At first it is unnoticed or

137

termed the "flu" or a "virus." Man looks for a potion to still his inward battle. This experience is the movement of his "sleeping" portion stirring and the dominant portion feeling a shift in its position.

The alteration of vibration is not introduced to man without his choosing, neither is it done "to" man by some outside source altering the energy pattern. Rather each time the quickening within man is experienced it is because one or ones have entered the dimension to bring about the initial thought or Divine Drop which activates the process.

One soul entering your dimension can begin such an activation or alteration of vibration. As you would speak of ones of your brethren who travel of the stars, so it is they too can enter of your dimension to carry the Divine Drop to begin a changing process. You, in your conscious state as you seek Truth, perpetuated the action. As numbers of ones increase the vibration, it is intensified and accelerated. Such a process is happening upon the planet known as Earth.

Initial Introduction Of The Divine Drops

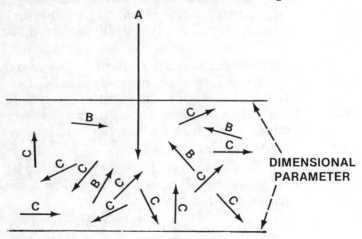

Figure 4

In the simple drawing (Figure 4) "A" represents the entrance of the Divine Drop. The arrows designated as "B" are the souls in the dimension who first feel of the change in vibration. They respond to the change. Others, "C," either are attracted to them or indicate no change in their behavior.

DIVINE
DROP

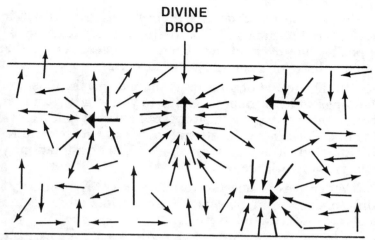

Figure 5

As the Divine Drop is experienced so it is some are attracted, some repelled and some choose to attempt maintenance of the existing vibration. This can be said of your dimension or it can be said of the individual.

See each arrow as an activity within your own cellular structure. The cosmic dance continues creating an ever changing, ever growing, ever expanding expression of the source of all creation, that which is known to you as God.

The form of the individual is a highly sensitive mechanism. It continually receives signals from its environs. One portion of the brain then translates these signals into messages which are either recorded in the consciousness or the unconsciousness. Ofttimes in your consciousness you register specific feelings, emotions or thoughts not recognizing where they have come from.

There are specific glands which will alter their functional level according to their signals. This can be demonstrated by the tingling one would feel on the nape of the neck. This is the physical registration of an energy which is not in harmony with yours, an indication of an energy which causes an intense unbalance.

Thus, all the body tenses, sensitivity heightens and one has increased strength to stand and face the unknown or the strength to bolt from the scene.

Have you not entered a room to feel the "vibes" in an uncomfortable manner? Or perhaps your reaction is the opposite, one of comfort? Have you ever met another to quickly discover a connection of fastness?

In this period of your cycle there are sensations, under-standings and experiences coming to you which seem pointed toward your own growth along your spiritual path. How can this be? Because of the alteration of your vehicle, added to the infusion of energies causing a further alteration, your awareness is heightened.

When it was selected to enter and stay primarily in a form/body within the earth's dimension other factors of evolvement/growth have their influence.

Where had this divine spark had most of its growth? What sphere exerted the greatest influence upon this one's growth?

Had the soul been on Earth, in its vibration, before? If so, how frequently? When was the last experience? Was the soul ready for the experience? Had it been scarred? Was the healing sufficient? Were the needed "other" ones going to be within this one's experience in this experience? What was the greatest potential for this one's own growth/evolvement?

Each one planning the earth experience considers these questions and many more for each earth experience has as its goal to express the divinity which is locked within it.

In addition to those ones who have entered into the earth vibration and are to grow within the experience, there are those who have come to join forces with the eartheans to assist in the changing process of your planet.

You call them the "star people" because they are not locked within the specific pattern of karma/dharma which you call life's experiences. Their purpose is to anchor the divine energies within the dimensional parameters of your dimension, to act as transmitters as the whole process is quickening. These ones seem to have a heightened sensitiv-ity to all about them. They have come as gifts to assist a planet of unsettled and confused brethren. They know of vibration and pulsation of energies. They are quick to note subtle differences which oft go unobserved by others.

Close examination of these ones would reveal there is a thinning of the wall of each cell of their being. The DNA/RNA factors of coding have a helix on the twelfth "rung" of the DNA. This helix alters the metabolism of the cell as well as its definition. (Earth scientists have yet to observe this process because they do not yet have the mechanisms to observe within the adomic level – that is the sub-sub-sub-atomic level.)

The alteration in cellular metabolism has impact upon all facets of the individual's existence including such things as activity tolerance, dietary preferences, susceptibility to invading organisms, attunement with vibrational patterns, altered mental capacities, etc.

These ones have been first to notice their personal absence of synchronization with the others who are so closely attuned with the Earth Mother. As they reach their adulthood, they reflect on being "different" as children. Though they wanted acceptance by their peers as children, they find as adults they continue to be responding to a rhythm different than the masses.

Most of these ones have a driving desire to "know," having difficulty accepting generalities. They seek for quietness and solitude to merely sit quietly reflecting or to read.

Their focus in life's occupation is to help others, to be of service. But once they have entered one of the service professions there is quick disillusionment with its acceptance of mediocrity.

In most instances, there is a longing within themselves which it seems cannot be satisfied. To meet another of similar vibration is as coming to an "oasis."

This place in your cycle is one in which ones are coming together, experiencing the energy shifts with joy. They find as they come together in small clusters there is an acceleration in their own process allowing them to begin their own understanding. Isolation and loneliness give way to purpose.

Those who seem more bound to a slower vibration appear unaffected by altered vibration or energy shifts. Why? It is because the DNA patterning of these ones, the soul's programing, is one more compatible with the slower vibration. These ones have had many facets of experience upon the plane of Earth. Their soul consciousness recognizes the choice of progression. The strength of each component of being in form is known from experience. The dominance of the physical, mental or other lead forces which will come forth and guide this portion of experience is known. The deity within recognizes the need for this expression in the balancing of the individual divine portion within the earth dimension.

Through the predetermined cycle of being, the vibration for the Earth Mother has become more finely tuned. This has been possible because of the acceptance and attunement of the "star" ones in form about the planet as they respond to more finely tuned vibrations.

This alteration in Earth's pattern, though gradual, has been experienced by those held in the cycle of rebirth. The relationship of Earth and her inhabitants is changing. Those who have been most closely bound with the slower vibration are feeling irritability, unbalance. Its origin cannot be defined, but nevertheless it remains intensifying through the whole facet of experience. The membrane of the cell's parameter is experiencing a decrease in the density about it. Activity within the call at its adomic level is initiating an alteration to the cell itself. Life is changing.

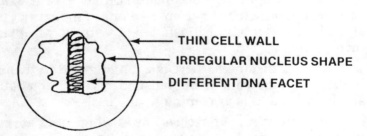

THIN CELL WALL
IRREGULAR NUCLEUS SHAPE
DIFFERENT DNA FACET

Figure 6

(1) The cellular pattern of the "star children" on planet Earth.

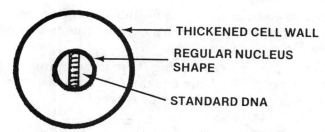

THICKENED CELL WALL

REGULAR NUCLEUS SHAPE

STANDARD DNA

(2) The cellular pattern of those who have many facets of experience with planet Earth.

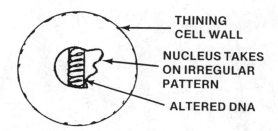

THINING CELL WALL

NUCLEUS TAKES ON IRREGULAR PATTERN

ALTERED DNA

(3) These same ones as they experience the change of the vibration of the Earth Mother.

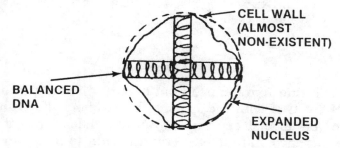

CELL WALL (ALMOST NON-EXISTENT)

BALANCED DNA

EXPANDED NUCLEUS

(4) The cellular structure of Earth man in the New Day (next cycle)

As "man" attunes to the changes in the energy vibration, he experiences a greater peace and awareness. The separation between him and all else decreases. This is the thinning of the walls of the cells. He, man, as the guiding influence upon the planet is the last to adjust to the vibration, for all of the creation aspects are attuning to the change. Man is "exercising" his duality as he struggles with each infusion.

143

Let us look at the energy infusion as it is received by Earth "mans kind," remembering that this is a continuous process since all began.

From the Source of Being there is a continuous flow of energy to assist all of the Creator/Creation aspects. Some might observe these as drops or waves or individual instances of great impact. Picture, if you will:

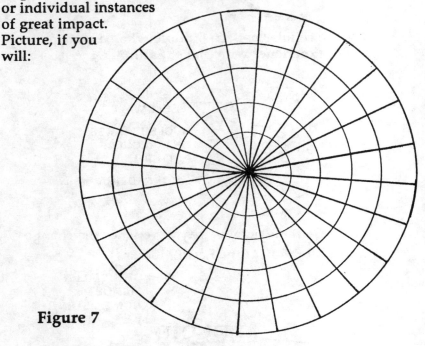

Figure 7

Each ring represents an out breath of Source, infusing that of creation with the spark to bring about life with the Creator facets that express the Source. Each straight line represents the continuous energy infusion to maintain that "level" or facet of creation. Each is continuous, composed of multiple drops.

For the purpose of this, assume Earth and its inhabitants are on the outer most ring. As Earth and its "mans kind" have grown – and all evolvement is a process of growing – each drop of infusion is experienced. Man, because of his place of primary experience, responds to one drop or particle more than another, just as each place on each circle responds according to its place in the overall growth process.

There are ones who feel no-thing or feel an agitation with a drop of infused energy. It is not theirs to acclaim but is to be acclaimed by those only who respond to it. Each drop of energy then as it reaches the utmost of expressed creation is drawn to begin a cycle of return to Source. This is a process of unending supply and acceptance. It is, perhaps, in the understanding of this concept that Earth man has felt of his going forth and returning to Source.

"Mans" on planet Earth – I speak of the collective representation of divine energy represented on the planet known to you as Earth – has come from many streams of evolution. At this place in the cycle, the representatives are as varied as their origin. Each has climbed to a particular rung of their DNA programming and is fired to experience and then express the deity within themselves.

The drop of energy as it is fused within Earth's dimension serves to assist in this process. Because of the presentation of duality, with its resultant set of experiences, the infusion is of varied reception.

As this portion was begun, we spoke of the taunting of the masculine and feminine – primarily the physical form – in this place on the cycle. Could this heightened sexual expression be motivated by the soul's desire to be the creator each has come to express, to present equally the gifts of each? The expression of the God facet within each is the purpose of experience. Man, as he experiences the dimension of duality, attempts to express himself in a variety of ways. Always, the leading force behind his action is the desire of the indwelling facet of Source to express its perfection.

As this desire pushes its way through the experience of life on planet Earth its expression oftimes appears quite at odds with the original purpose. Different components take on the lead force role and present that interpretation of the desire of the deity within. "Mans kind" on planet Earth comes to the close of a cycle.

The deity within presses for expression. According to the lead force of the individual it will come forth in a variety of ways. The stimulation of the basic drive of creation is not sexual laxity but rather the desire of the soul to express the creator facet in its creative process.

Beloved brethren of the planet known as Earth, be the creator facet only you can express. Allow your portion of Source to be at its fullest. Let no-thing deter you. Welcome each drop of the infusion according to your own resonance pattern, growing with the experience.

I bless you. I bless the God within you. I bless the expression of that God.

I am One Drop of the Cosmic Christ.

(Received thru Tuieta of the Emerauld Cross, of the Golden Robe.)
Copyright 1991, Portals of Light, Inc.
P.O. Box 15621, Fort Wayne, IN 46885

Chapter 10

Pallas Athena and AEolus

Channeled by Bob Fickes

It is with great joy and great love in our hearts that we greet you once again. We bring forth this teaching of old and yet of new. It is a teaching of the ancients, for it is the awakening of the ancient soul. It is the awakening of the ancient gift of God to every human being on Earth.

We are AEolus and also Pallas Athena, divine complements, Fullness and Freedom. We bring to you, therefore, those things that are indeed the gift of God and the Light of the Holy Spirit. For we are Masters of the Ray of the Holy Spirit, what you would call the White Light and the Freedom Flame. We bring forth to you then that which is perfect freedom, agility, and that which complements Heaven.

The subject of Ascension is a most interesting, exciting and delightful process for us to discover with you. For indeed, as we would see, you are ascended already! And that we know to be true. We would also recognize within you, the seat of the Soul in the Heart, and how, even now, the Master sits upon the throne of the Heart that you are, and welcomes your every wish and commands it to be so.

But in that which is the folly of human life and its experience, there is often a time when you do not know what you desire nor what you request of this great and holy Master, whose throne is in the Heart. For in truth, that which is your own heart does not understand life, for it is surrounded by many other authorities to which you have given your power.

And I say to you now, command that which is the Commander in Chief of all authorities. You shall know Infinite and Perfect Peace. You shall know perfection even whilst on Earth. All of these things are at your disposal. They are timely, they would meet with you in good order and according to right time.

All of these things that we speak about, dear ones, are the commands that you have given to all authorities on Earth. If that command be "I am your servant," then you are the servant of those things that are here to serve you.

We welcome you with this understanding of perfect truth, for it is an understanding of life itself. The I AM That I AM is the Commander in Chief, not your human ego, nor its perceptions, for your human ego and its perceptions are built from the very bonds that confine you. It is the limitation of self that you have learned to experience and to accept as life itself!

Let Thy bonds be broken! And let Thy Soul ascend like a Silver Dove into Heaven!

I would ask that each of you now close your eyes and be filled with the Light of the Holy Spirit. May the very Presence of God in your heart, the I AM That I AM, accelerate, blowing fast upon the Freedom Flame so that it no longer simply flickers and dies out, but grows strong and luminous within the spinal column and the entire body of your being.

May all that which is already ascended be known! And I call forth within that which is your own being of Light, that Ascended Master bodily form that you already are! That you may know this form, that it may greet you, and that it may bring you mastery whilst on Earth!

Each of you, my chelas, open your eyes now from within your heart, and you will see that Master That You Are, there before you, luminous as a Holy Angel of God. Each of you is possessed of such a Soul as to achieve greatness. Each of you has that opportunity now laying before you to ascend! Each of you has a Holy Master to guide you that is your own I AM Presence! And there luminous before you He or She now stands!

I would have you to understand that this luminous Soul, this great being of Light and this Master whom you have called is, indeed, a manifestation on a physicalized and dimensional level, an interdimensional level of perception, a concretized image of your own I AM Presence.

This Master form will take on the personality to whom you are most guided, to worship and to feel benevolence from, and compassion and wisdom. You may be experiencing this Master as something other than your I AM Presence, perhaps a Presence that you have known or associated with – even another Master on Earth.

Do not be confused by this, dear ones, for this loving form with which you are presented, in fact, actualizes a part of your own being. Do not mistake appearances, dear ones, for these appearances are merely the projections of your own Soul, your I AM Presence! It will, in manifesting itself to you, take on whatever form you desire. It will bring to you acceptance and love and wisdom teachings in the form of whatever benevolent Master you require.

For in point of fact, that Master is referenced by you as a result of your own love for Self, for that which is Divine within you mirrors this great Soul of which you are reminded on Earth.

Each of you possesses such a memory as to go beyond your conscious mind. You will be drawn to certain circumstances and elevated states of consciousness that will remind you of that which you possess in your I AM Presence as Infinite Wisdom, Infinite Peace, Infinite Love!

Each of you, then, throughout your lifetime, will be drawn to circumstances and individuals and teachings, Masters far wiser than yourselves who are in truth only a part of yourself and reflect the perfect spirit of your Inner Being. This spirit is the I AM Presence.

We call on you to embrace this Holy Spirit that now stands before you, for it is your own I AM! It is your own Divinity of Self! Embrace this form with this Master present and know it to be your guide and teacher, for you are the students and your Higher Selves are your Masters!

Put aside the form of human ego and its captive mind, and allow yourselves to embrace the Infinite Wisdom that your I AM Presence possesses. Bring forth out of Spirit those things that you are, and bring them forth through the teachings of the heart in the fond embrace of your favorite Master form that stands before you now!

Do you not feel an exhilaration and a quickening? This is the first stage of Ascension, for that which is the heart and core of life in the physical and material dimension of Earth begins to quicken, to lighten, to accelerate as a form of God is presented to it. Already the bonds that have ensnared you have begun to be broken.

What is the bond? What is its snare? It is the captive existence of human ego. It is the form that you willingly gave to this Earth and to Earth authority. In so doing, you relinquished some of your own liveliness and life force. In so doing, that liveliness and life force began a process of decelerating, of slowing down its vibration, and condensating even as steam into water, and water into ice!

As this form becomes quickened, however, the process is reversed. You begin a return to your origin. The word "religion" meaning bending back, is a teaching that brings all souls back home. Home is where the Heart is. And the Heart is where God is. And a reminder of God brings a quickening to the Heart. As the Heart accelerates, a communication is sent forth to every cell of the body.

This communication is first registered by the brain and by the various organs of the body as a sensation of acceleration or quickening. Often you will feel such a quickening as just a shiver or chill. Many of you have requested that your bodies give you signs when a truth is heard. You will find this manifesting in a number of ways, as what you call chicken skin or goose bumps, as what you would call a rush of light, a flash of light, a sensation or feeling of exhilaration. Though only for a moment, this is the Light that quickens and liberates.

Each of you on Earth possess such insight and power, for it was yours in the beginning, is now, and ever shall be yours. It is a world without end! The end is only the illusion of the human mind as it chooses one thing over another, turning its back upon the former and moving on. An end appears to have occurred. But there is no end in God, for all of those things that you are continue for lifetimes. Even where you have turned your back upon them they reappear. Life is endless, and all of those things which you once have manifested will return to you. They are all completing now. They are completing their cycles. The endless repetitions of human karma are all returning home. Their wheels are spinning homeward bound. And every soul on Earth participates in this glorious and illustrious event!

In the next ten years of your Earth's future, all souls on Earth will be guided home. Many souls will choose to remain where they are for a while longer; they will be given an opportunity to do so. But the Earth vibration and planet itself shall remain homeward bound.

Therefore those students of life who would wish to linger in the field of karma will be given an opportunity to share that life of karma with others not of Earth's origin. They shall be given this opportunity through a variety of means, to return to another dimension and to experience Earthly karma in that dimensional point of view.

But all of those souls who wish to remain with Earth must understand that they are on a ship gliding through space whose timewarp is now accelerating into the highest dimensional experience possible. It is for you to recognize and to understand that all of Earth is a planet in transition, and that all souls associated with Earth are a part of that transition.

You cannot exclude any dimension of your own body from any experience that you would have, for every part of your body participates in that experience. Even so does every part of Earth participate in the Ascension Plan, whether they prefer it, whether they have chosen it consciously or not. All have chosen in spirit to return home one day, and that day has come! And this decade is a day in the eye of God.

All souls are returning home.

A great feast has been prepared for each one of you. A feast that was yours in the beginning, is now, and ever shall be yours as you come forth into your own being. Many teachers will greet you from both unseen planes and physical planes. They will express their knowledge to you, that knowledge which your own I AM Presence has requested.

Often you will not be ready for this knowledge. It is there simply to inform you and to prepare you. Each stage has its own receptivity, and the first stage is rejection, though it hears the words. And after that the heart begins to quicken and to melt its boundaries and its confinements, its own limitations and authorities that it has placed around itself. As the very walls and armors of the heart begin to release and to melt down, the Ascended Flame will consume all illusions, and the brightness that shines forth will reveal only truth.

God has said that He will come to test the materials of your labors, and the Great Flame shall come forth out of Heaven and consume that which you have made. Those things that were made in Heaven shall last, and those things that were made of Earth shall be consumed, and then, at that time, all that remains will be of God.

You will mourn under your labors and your losses, for in the beginning it will appear to you as though all is lost, but in the end all has been gained. That which once protected and armored you, now has been released and the very Flame of God has been ignited. For what was once seen as a protection will later be seen as an armored wall that separates you from the very loved ones that you call in Heaven.

Blessings to you, I AM AEolus together with Pallas Athena. We greet you with a message of Ascension and information to teach you the Ascension Process. This has been the first phase of that Teaching, to acknowledge your I AM Self and Its Presence, to have it embody a form before you that you might recognize It has a Master Teacher.

Perhaps in the beginning it is better for your will to understand this Master as separate from self, but in the end, later, with your development, you will learn to understand this Master as your Self with no separation between you. You will see your true form, the I AM Presence that you are, and the Fullness that God gave to you in the beginning. As it is now, you labor under the burden of a physical body that is cumbersome by nature. In addition, you are carrying the weight of your ancestors of many generations.

All of your ancestors' authorities are borne by this body and accepted by the human ego that inhabits it. All of their forms of belief are embodied within the cells of this body, embedded in the DNA. On a very practical note, however, all of that which is called the cellular composition of the body is made of Light, and, therefore, those beliefs are all illusion, changeable at any moment. But because they have been placed there a generation at a time, we see you, too, laboring under them and under their weight and strain. It is as though your mind were in a vise-grip of attention, holding fast to the beliefs of your ancestors and to your society. Your human mind holds to these beliefs, as if, were it to release them, it would surely die or perish, or some unseen force would come and take it away.

Dear Children of Light, we have a message of great importance for you to hear: *There is no physical force in this universe, save your own, that can take you away without your willingness to go.*

That is why we say there is no form in Earth or Heaven that can take you away. You are that God, and that God-presence dwells within you. Without It your very lifeforce would be extinguished. For that very lifeforce, infinitely small, is the power of God indeed!

It was your Christ that spoke to you with the words of Faith. Faith the size of a grain of mustard that could move even a great mountain, that Faith is the Flame of Life. Though It is infinitely small, and the mountain of your karma and its physical body seems infinitely large, even Faith the size of a grain of mustard can move that mountain of karma. It is the lifeforce that is a part of you that can quicken. Many of you have seen a campfire that once existed and now exists only as an ember. One glowing ember is enough to remember God. And to remember God is enough to fan the ember to create the flame.

One tiny flame is enough to ignite all of Creation and create a bonfire of rejoicing.

Blessed ones, do not give up hope. Faith is your weapon against illusion. It is the only triumph, for faith fans the Flame of Life! Your ego will try to confine that Flame as it burns. It will build a wall around it, trying to protect itself and all that it owns. But a Flame, once burning brightly, must consume all things until only the Flame remains.

In the end, All is God, and all of those things which you would love would stand before Him and as you would see, all of those things do stand in His way. For were you yet to place your attention upon them, you would not have your attention upon Him.

This is understood only by the wise, for there are many who would make an illusion of Him and create false gods. These false gods do not necessarily have to be idolatry, formed in statues and the like. They are your very concepts and beliefs that form these statues in the first place. They can be as obvious and as simple as that which you call your leader, whom you worship and praise, or the dollar bill in your purse, or they can be as subtle as the very beliefs that you carry about God. Authorities come in many shapes and sizes, and all of which detract from the message of God to the human soul.

I AM the Light. I AM the Way. These were the words of your Christ. This Christ reminded you of that gift of Christ within you. The Christ within you is God in Motion. It is the Living and Awakened God. It is the Living and Awakened I AM.

As this Flame of the I AM Presence starts to quicken, It grows luminously large and beautiful. It receives of Compassion and Grace. Grace is the outpouring or outflowing of God into human life, into all avenues of life. It is the cup that runneth over. And even though it walks in the very shadows of death, in a field of illusion, and a world of forms and authorities, yet, the staff is strong and the wind will not bend it or break it.

As the Flame of Life becomes fanned, as the quickening accelerates, the human body responds, first with a shiver, and then with a sustained vibration of acceleration and quickening. Your breath and your heart will both quicken. The heart beating in the chest and the breath accelerating, you will feel a whirlwind of energy within you, within the very breath that you breathe. And as that breath expands and continues to reach each cell of the body, the quickening continues, until a pulsation is felt throughout the entire physical form.

You will notice a mighty river growing in your spine, for this is the staff. It is the staff of Life. It is the Tree of God. It is the sephiroth and the kundalini. They are all the same. It is the quickening of this Tree of Life that will magnetize to it everything that it must consume. All illusions must become transparent until Truth remains only. As the quickening process accelerates, the Tree of Life, the Staff becomes strong. You will feel the energy of Light within the spine connecting both heart and mind, soul and body together. It will move up and down the spine, until all parts of Self are recognized.

Wheresoever there is darkness within the human form, then the Light must penetrate there more carefully. For these are areas of your own personality that you have hidden from your view. These are areas that you have chosen by your authorities not to gaze upon, for they did not suit your reality upon the Earth. But this would be much like that which is the room of clutter that you hide from your neighbor's view. Perhaps it is an attic or basement, perhaps a closet in which you have chosen to hide your belongings that you wish for others not to view, including yourself.

These darkened places must be recognized, however, dear ones. They must become illuminated, and the first sight of them would bring you fear and would cause you concern. But on the path of the quickening, first there is acceleration and love, and then the flame becomes more dangerous and bold as it moves headlong into those experiences that you would not wish to share with others.

In this time period you will be challenged by many forces of authority. And know dear ones, these forces of authority are all self-made, and that they are all illusions created by your own soul and its choices.

The I AM Presence is the Commander that would welcome all of your requests and honor them. Even where you would place greater authority elsewhere, it would give that gift to you. For whatever your desire, the I AM Presence must create. Where you give your authority to another, It must create it. Where you acknowledge that which is your own power, It also must create it. And where you acknowledge both, It also must create it. It will bring to you guiding soul experiences of either challenge or benevolence, depending upon your persuasion.

The soul is always being guided by your I AM Presence, even when it seems to you that it is not. It is a gift that comes to you from God. These experiences are meant to shake you and awaken you. They are meant to challenge and to shake out your fear, for where there is no fear in the heart, there is no illusion. Where there is illusion, however, there shall be fear.

What do we mean by this? Fear is born of illusion. When you have created a false authority, one which you inevitably lose, you will innately be afraid of its loss. Dear ones, those things which you fear are born of your illusions, for you understand in your heart that you will lose them.

Fear is the knowingness that you have placed your authority and emphasis elsewhere than in God.

It is to be said that all fear is born illusion. When you recreate Truth in your hearts, by fanning the Freedom Flame, then you recreate the knowingness of God in your heart and there shall be no fear. This trepidation is felt by every soul on Earth. And as the body of Light becomes cleansed of its darkness and illusion, its false gods and authorities, each soul of Earth shall undergo a transformation.

Sometimes it is possible for the soul to accept God all at once. In that great and triumphant moment, however, the quickening becomes almost insurmountable, impossible to control. It is as though it accelerates the very soul out of the body, and one loses the experience of Earthly reality.

This experience, which is called an out of body experience by most of you (by others it would be called an acceleration into the Transcendent where no physical form remains, only the Light of God), must be anchored and brought back. It must be brought into the soul and into the physical form. In fact what has taken place is that your own awareness could not sustain itself in such Light and Power. It became lost. That awareness willingly and gratefully becomes lost in God.

However, what was lost must be found again, and usually at the expense of losing God. And so the pendulum will swing from such God experiences to human reality. You will feel in one moment exhilarated and the next confined. You will feel the freedom taken away from you, only to be remembered and to be praised. But, dear ones, the pendulum will swing back and forth again and again.

Our caution and our recommendation is for each one of you to be aware throughout all of the quickening motion of your physical form, its body and its awareness, its heart and soul. As the quickening process accelerates within you, leave not this body behind, but take it with you. This is the definition of Ascension, that you are not to leave behind those things which you have made, but you should create them now with Heaven's tools. This means that which has become physical and condensed will now melt down and transform. The very material and substance of the human body will be caused to be made of Light.

As Jesus accomplished this task, an image was created on the cloth that surrounded His body. The electromagnetic chemicalization that took place in His physical form was so immense and spectacular in that moment that it left an image in the shroud. Today it is well known that such a shroud exists. Whether it is the shroud that you possess already or another, does not matter. The Truth has become illuminated. That which was Jesus' shroud does exist and its power, the power that it holds from the transformation of ascension is an inspiration for all to behold.

Each one of you will undergo a similar process, perhaps not in the three day time period that it took Jesus to create His ascension, but it shall be over a longer period of time that your bodies will ascend. They have already begun this process with each quickening. Each quickening shifts the awareness and attunes the cells. Each DNA structure becomes altered when a current of Light passes through it.

The illusions of before shall be overcome as the sun grows brighter. A false god can only be seen as truth when the light is dim. But when it is that the sun glows brightly, you recognize each soul on Earth as a soul like your own. No greater, no less than. All equal in the eyes of God. And whatsoever authorities they have given to you, you have given to them. They are entrusted with that gift, but they are neither better or worse than yourself.

We would have you to understand then, with this realization, that they cannot serve you ultimately in finding the Kingdom of God or creating His Kingdom on Earth. Only you can do this, for only your soul has the power of the I AM. That I AM Presence is present for your self and your self alone. And were you to be one of those compassionate souls to give gifts to others of healing, we say to you call upon their I AM Presence to acknowledge this healing, for as each of you have recognized, you cannot heal another unless they are willing to heal themselves. In truth no soul on Earth heals another save God within each one of them.

Blessings to you then, dearest ones, for we have begun now the second phase instruction, that which is the reconstruction of physical form out of the quickening process. This, too, has many stages: one – the illumination lasts longer and in that process a quickening continues to release and to shake free the illusions that bind. The confinements of the human ego and their authorities are to melt away as one begins to perceive them for what they are, merely separations of inanimate matter.

We see that inanimately becoming more animate with the Light and Power of your own I AM Presence. We see the garment wrapped around the Soul now being unraveled, as the Light and Power of the Mighty I AM Presence becomes illuminated.

The DNA was condensed, dear ones, about the Soul. It was lifted and transformed by the very illusions that you carry in your human ego. What was once simply thought has now become matter, the material of the universe of form.

How was that form created? How was thought crystallized into form? The generations of your ancestors, created over time that which you know as genetics. The power of their thought did it. It was the authority created in them, strong enough to create the threads of reality known to you as genes.

These genes yet carry the thoughts and feelings of your ancestors, and as they begin to melt from the heat of the quickenings, they will appear one by one to your view, even as they did to those who came before you.

The closets of the DNA are open now and all transformations include the gene pool, or shall we say the melting of old authorities carried by them. It is this melting process, the coming alive of the inanimate, encrusted thought forms, that shall liberate the Soul from its hiding place.

This begins then a new phase and a new quickening, for the embodiments of old will now be liberated. No form will remain the same. You have traveled through time on a spiral staircase, traveling downwards into the third dimension of reality. With each step you lowered your vibration, condensed of your form, and limited of the very essence of your power. You wrapped the cloth of belief about yourself and called it home, encasing your Soul forever. You knew each of your ancestors in advance and saw them coming. You embraced them and called them home or family. You wrapped their clothes about you and forgot of your essence and your name.

Now you live in a masked identity, covered by the travels of your ancestors, imprisoned by the controls they bestowed on you. Where once you lived with Infinity and with God, now you live with limitation and death. Your illusions lasting only a hundred years or more. Your bodies have become statues of living memories re-enacting the experiences of your past.

Soon you will be completing this journey and be called home. There you will be perfect again with the Father/Mother of All Creation. You will live in the Garden of Beauty where your form will last forever in the Light.

You are on this journey now, and remembering where you have been. The records of the past have not been known to you until now. The veils have all been lifted, and the knowledge of the journey of humankind has been open to you. It tells you of your future even as it describes where you have been in your past. The journey of Atlantis and Lemuria will all be open to you, the memory of things long forgotten. Four and a half million years of physical descending from light into matter is involved. Your cells remember this process and now return.

Liberate yourselves (your cells) from these experiences

now as we take you on a journey back towards your link with heaven. Liberate your heart and mind from the grip of Earthly power, so that the realignment and reconstruction of the physical form may begin.

Each cell becomes attuned to whatever quality of light will pass through it. Your cells have all been modified and will be modified many times more, depending upon the current and frequency of your vision and life force. Each of you will determine this for yourself.

Thus far, the majority of you have determined to create a third dimension. The third dimensional point of view is one of limitation and death, a limitation to your human freedom, and a condensation into physical reality. This condensation into physical reality has had certain appropriate measurements, these determinable by your limited science. But as the frequencies of life become more accelerated and quickened, the very physical cells will begin to reorganize and repattern themselves. Your chromosomes and DNA will all begin to be altered. There will be no memory of a past. There will only be its illusion. That which will be the illusion shall be a transparent form, like a narrow shell.

To experience this, close your eyes and call forth the Infinite Light from your I AM Soul or Presence within you. Now ask that your Master Consciousness step inside of you and embody that which is your physical form. As It does so feel the quickening and the acceleration, the dimensional shift in your perception as It goes beyond your limits.

Allow the Light to spread and to shine clear of any resistance. Release those resistances now! Let them go as the Light will pass through them. Light has the infinite capacity to travel anywhere It likes. There is no physical form that can restrict Light. In some measure, in some way, a photon will pass through even the most solid object. So it is that as your own awareness stretches, you will stretch beyond your limitations into that which is the Infinite Light.

Let the Infinite Light grow strong and let that which is Its universal application be known by you. As the Light I AM shines within you, the Infinite God shines with you. The Light that you are, is the Light of God. The Light of God has always shone within your own life force. You are a part of God. *You are a cell in the Infinite Being.*

As you acknowledge your own Infinitude, you acknowl-edge that you are Infinitely Present and Wise. All Time is within your hand. To grasp this is to understand Infinite Wisdom and Potential. It is to rest in the Heart of God, which is the seat of your own heart.

Recognize now, that as the Light shines brightly, it seems to overtake and stretch beyond the form that you identified as self. You begin to see that your own form is but a chalice to hold the nectar of God. You begin to understand that you are this Light, and that the chalice is but the container.

This is the first recognition of the dimension of percep-tion called the fourth dimension. For here it is that your own confusion about the nature of Life is finally dissolved and you recognize that you are Light, and Light is your True Form.

You yet perceive the chalice, however, and know it to be real. But from your own dimensional point of view as you enter into the fourth dimension, it is as though the third dimension only holds or houses that which is the Light. The Light is who you are.

Who is the chalice, and how is it formed? It was formed and possessed of all the authorities that you have given to it. For each request that you have given to your Mighty I AM Presence, the Commander in Chief, would create a form for you. And with each form that was created, another brick was added to the structure of the physical body.

The physical body itself is a structure like any building, created out of your thoughts. And as each thought is mounted upon the other, it creates a physical form for you to inhabit. It will protect you against whatever elements you have chosen to dwell in. It will chose those things wisely that you would need in advance. Your own physical forms will adapt to weather conditions and to personality condi-tions. All of the systems that you will engage in, your personality self will create, and bricks will be added to the body to protect you.

This is the chalice that you have formed. It can also be known as a chariot for the Light of the Soul. And when it is that the chariot can no longer sustain the abuses of physical life and becomes broken down, it is discarded for another. But the Soul Itself is eternal. It was given that gift by God.

Now, as a fourth dimensional being, or a being entering the fourth dimension, you begin to understand that you are this Infinite Light and Its Infinite Potential, and you yet have a chalice in which to perform. We say to you now, view this chalice with even more Light! And you begin to see that it is not solid but composed only of thoughts and perceptions. It becomes transparent, as though paper thin. Even as you witness it, you see that you are beyond your own condition.

This is a more accelerated form of the fourth dimension, for in its higher stages the chalice itself becomes more transparent so that it is just barely visible to your eyes. In this way, however, you will learn to accept that you are the Infinite God and that the Mighty I AM Presence is your gift.

We say to you, each of you have a task to perform on behalf of God. For every cell in God's body has His Infinity and His Infinite Purpose. All cells will spontaneously cooperate with one another as they become realigned with the truth of God in them, for they are all one motion.

Were you to be physically embodied in anything other than the image of God, we would see the cells of your body all traveling in different directions and you would not survive. You would literally fall apart in a million pieces! And no Life Force would be remaining to hold you together.

But the Life Force that holds you together is named Love. And Love is the Grace and Goodness of God that unites all things. Even were they to begin to separate, Love would bring them back. Love is the charm of Life. Love is the power by which all this universe is held together.

Before Love came faith. Out of that Faith came the power of the Quickening, and that Quickening Flame began to express Itself as Existence. Out of that then, there was what can be seen as Hope.

For from that which is called the Power, Hope emerges. Hope that is the Presence of God. Hope that is the Perception that the Light passes beyond its own condition. Hope that the Light will eventually triumph and its power become Infinite. Hope that the Quickening Process will create Ascension, and Eternal Life will be given to you, even in physical form. Hope that all that you are will become one with God again. And This, then, becomes Love!

Love is the choice that creates the fifth dimension when all things become united!

Whilst you are yet in the fourth dimension, however, we would have you to perceive form outside the body. There you will recognize the chalice still holds the Light. And you will see that even though the chalice has become transparent to your vision, it yet is solid to another's.

You will recognize that even as you pass through life knowing who you are as the Infinite God, yet others will perceive you as an individual, will understand your ways as they would see them. Therefore they would not always know of your Wisdom, for their eyes cannot perceive You. They only perceive the chalice!

This is a perception of the fourth dimension: In the first phase of Ascension, which is to take place in this decade, all Souls of Light will recognize themselves as Light. Their chalice will begin to transform and the electromagnetic patterns realign. All things will become synchronized with God once again, and all the Infinite Patterns of the universe will be explored. The vision, however, of the chalice will remain somewhat the same.

You will not yet ascend into full Light in the way in which you might imagine as all of Earth dissolving and being physical no more. No, you will yet have a physical existence, but it will be fourth dimensional existence, one in which the duality of life is shared, in which all of Light becomes known to you, and all of physical existence shares knowingly in that Light and becomes modified.

The modification and reconstruction process of your planet Earth will begin in the later portion of this decade, as all of the systems of the Earth become realigned to Truth. This is also part of the physical ascension that must take place in this Day of God (this decade).

In the first portion of the Day, it is as though the soul awakens and sees the Light dawning. But as the dawn gets brighter and brighter, and the full noon now becomes explored, all the things that were hidden will be revealed. By 1995 or 96 of your years counting, there shall be such explorations of hidden things, that nothing will remain unexposed. In that time period then the Light must shine in such a way as to recompute the systems of the Earth, to reformulate them, to reconstitute them to be in harmony with the Infinite God and the Infinite Wisdom of the universe. The Light must flow one to the other and flow harmoniously without friction. All of your sciences will embrace a science of friction free superfluid conductivity, all things in harmony with each other.

In addition to this, your own physical forms shall be transformed and re-embodied. They will be re-embodied with Spirit, with the spiritual essence and dimensions of who you are. This will be the completion of third dimensional transition into the fourth dimension of ascension.

As for the physical reconstituting of the body into complete light, this will take approximately another two thousand years. So it shall be that as the third dimension took two thousand years to complete of itself once it had determined to do so with the birth of Jesus on Earth, now it will do so again with the rebirth of the Christ in every Soul, for the fourth dimension is the Second Coming.

It is the coming of the Christ Child within each chalice. It is the Light of the Living God overflowing the chalice even in the shadow of death, until all that which is death is seen as an illusion, a transparent reality which once held lordship over the Soul because the Soul's authority was given to it. Now the Soul must reclaim its own authority and that ascension process reconstituted and begun.

I welcome you now into that which is the agency of Love. Sit back and breathe once more the Light that you are, the Light beyond the chalice and visualize! Visualize those things that you love one by one being embraced by you. As they are embraced by you and the Light, they become more than the chalice, they become the Light Itself. Indeed, all of those things that you would love so dearly, would melt and be consumed by the Light I AM.

This Light of the God I AM, the God Presence, and the Inner Christ will embrace everything until all things become a part of you, a part of God I AM once again. All of Life will become consumed in this way.

Embrace them all one by one. That one that you love so dearly, bring him or her into your heart until they, too, become One Light. Those children and those gifts that are around you, bring them in to that Light until they, too, become One. Those parents and friends, bring them in before you, one by one, in order of love's appearance, until they, too, become One. Those things on which you sit, those things for which your body has been endowed, those things that surround you in the room, in the house, bring them in until they, too, become One.

All Light sustains everything in the universe. And all things in the universe are all Light. Bring now the cloud of illusion of your past into the Light, and it becomes One.

Bring now the surrounding atmosphere, the houses, the buildings, the forms of human lives, the automobiles, and all the machineries of life, bring them in. Your entire city brought into the heart and into the Light, and it, too, becomes One.

Bring now your troubled nation and its perspective of the world into your heart, into the Light, and it, too, becomes Light. See all the troubles and concerns of your national heritage being brought into the Light, so that the tremors that they have created on your human forms might be dissolved with Love. This is Infinite Love, my friends, this is Infinite Love!

Bring them all into this Love and they become One with Light. Bring now your unhealthy Earth into this Light, so that all of those things that are of Nature are brought into the Love. They will be infinitely responsive and rejoice. You will see them become excited and a quickening take place. The Earth shall quicken itself into completion and into perfection, and all the environmental ills shall be healed, as though over night. Bring them into the Light and they will all become One.

And all the national boundaries now, bring into your Light that they might become One, One Earth, One Perception, One Love of God. Bring the entire Earth now and Her body with all of its people and all of its beliefs, all its heavens and all astral worlds into the Light, and it, too, becomes One with the Light. And bring now all of Earth's brothers and sisters, who are waiting for you in Heaven, for all of the planets of this Solar System have all ascended and are waiting for you in the fourth dimension. Bring them in, until they, too, become One and you are reunited in Peace and Brotherhood.

Now we see the path and course of time that in the next two thousand year sequence not only will Earth become Light, but all this Solar System will ascend into the Pure Light. There will be no physical universe, as you understand it, to your perception in two thousand years. It will be all One.

It will be a Light World freed of any density, any limitation. All of life shall be the Infinite Life and the Infinite Joy of God. It will be sustained through the current of Love that joins all things together and it shall be growing by the Grace of God, which is the momentum of God's desire through the I AM Presence in every heart.

Blessings to you! These experiences represent to you the transition from third dimension to fourth dimension in this Day of God (this decade), and the two thousand year sequence to the fifth dimension.

The final phase of fifth dimension is the operation of all things as Light. The entire Solar System will join with that which is the Light of its True Form. There will be no physical Solar System as you recognize it in two thousand years; it shall return to its full velocity as Light.

Each Soul on Earth and all the systems of planets will have accepted that condition as their own. They will re-embrace that which is their God-maker. All things will return to their origin. You are ready, dear ones, to ascend into the fourth dimension in this Day of God.

I AM AEolus, together with Pallas Athena, and we welcome you with this vision of Ascension. A vision of Ascension that brings to you the most completeness and perfection that you have ever known or cherished. Let go of those things which confine you now and trust in the motion of God. Once that Flame has been ignited, It shall consume all things in Its path until no illusion remains, only Light!

I AM That I AM. And all of Life is before ME. Blessings to you.

Chapter 11

The Pleiadians

Channeled by Barbara J. Marciniak

We are here. It is our pleasure to be in your reality once again, particularly at this time. We are gathered together to have a good time and give informative data to be published upon your planet. These publications can awaken and affect codes of consciousness of the masses. When these words that will come through us and are gathered as a cooperation of ideas, a cooperative codicil of consciousness for the evolving humans, the readers will respond by having their codings fired when they see in print what is stored inside of them as deep knowings. Many publications, concepts and ideas are being broadcast to your planet that are ideas that are stored and coded inside of the DNA.

One thing that the human race has in common with one another is that they share a belief system. Within that belief system there is incredible richness and variety. Yet, it is a belief system in which the Earth is an agreed-upon boundary that binds the human race together.

This Earth is a compilation of energies and consciousness designed to house what would be called experiments, very much the same way that you would build a civic auditorium to hold events. The Earth designed and appropriated its existence in order to house, sponsor and hold experiments of consciousness. All planets are designed with a purpose. Your planet Earth creates an arena to house living forms of energy, animate forms of energy intricately laced with a web-work of consciousness that is filled with the history of your existing system called the Living Library. We wonder if those who will be reading these words will be ready to receive the catapult in consciousness caused by the concepts we bring.

Earth, if you can conceive of this, was to be a Living Library, an intergalactic exchange center for information, a locale existing within your galactic system that would act as a link-up, a beam center, a storehouse of information. It would tell the tale of conscious and cooperative adventures, and perhaps, conscious and uncooperative adventures, as they have unfolded in the history of your Universe.

It was an undertaking of tremendous magnitude to bring about a coalition of cooperation where all sentient beings would contribute the sum of their knowledge and work together. They would create a place where that knowledge could bring about something brand new in the realms of entertainment to bring about pleasure for all of those who would create.

Genetically speaking, evolved energies began to contribute the wealth of their own knowledge. We speak of energies that were capable of existing in multitudes of realities. The coordination of this kind of knowledge needed to be transduced because the knowledge was viable, real, in many different systems. Some systems were unaware of the existence of other systems. How to get all of this variety of knowledge and where to create a platform that it could exist in cooperation? This was the original plan and design of the Earth: a place where data and knowledge would be stored and where beings with the proper visas could obtain direct knowledge and experience of the stored information from the entire Universe. Even in this free will zone there had to be certain avenues that were utilized in order to enter this realm of stored knowledge.

Think for a moment, and then feel what we are discussing here. The words that we choose, the concepts we bring, are concepts that are stored deep inside of the body. They wait for the questions to be posed to your bodies so that you can begin to resonate with the answers inside of yourselves. Then the cellular memory within the body begins to remember what it already knows as we speak of it.

Back to this concept of the Living Library. This pooled knowledge was gathered together and, biogenetically all substances were engineered to have consciousness. Each conscious entity was engineered so that the composition of all existence on this planet would be threaded with data. Remember, we are saying consciousness is within all things – in the soil, in the rocks, in the trees, in the water, in all things.

On a microcosmic level tiny fibers that we call light-encoded filaments, carry information. These fibers were designed by these incredible Original Planners of this, your particular Earth. They were designed to react and to interact with one another. In other words, one form of knowledge was able to trigger off knowledge within another by interacting, by seeing, by touching, by tasting. Those senses are presently distorted in you; however, in the past you activated the Living Library by simply *being*.

The Living Library, in its own evolution, underwent many raids and changes of administrations. There were those who eventually took over the Living Library and, to a certain extent, disassembled and quarantined it. It's been kept hidden away so that in certain planes of existence your Earth has been long forgotten. Only in these last few decades has your Earth been rediscovered by those other planes of existence. Increased UFO activity is a direct result of an intention of reactivating certain portions of the Living Library.

Your Earth is presently moving very rapidly toward playing a major part in a tremendously cosmic universal drama. When a planetary sphere, a planetary home, is sponsoring or hosting events of such magnitude, many come from far and wide to participate. This is not a small event, but an integral part of a very gigantic plan that is set about to move energies in very different packages throughout the Universe and galaxy.

Your Earth is at a key point. Whenever key points are opened, energies of seemingly opposing factions are drawn together to create the drama. You see, you exist in a world where polarities feed you data about yourselves. An increase in the electromagnetic vibratory rate is occurring for all existence within this sphere of activity. The human evolutionary process has required that mankind must create something outside of themselves which explains their own inner workings.

Mankind is evolving because you are being triggered from outside of yourselves. That triggering from outside is specifically designed by beings who are orchestrating the reactivation of the Living Library. Within the Living Library are energies that contain the complete history of your Universe. This center of existence is being taken over once again by those who originally designed it so that stored information would be free to those who had visas to access it. It was not just for a privileged few; it was for many.

This liberating information is now being reawakened as a necessary activity to change the movement of the entire Universe towards a greater evolutionary understanding of its own existence on a universal level, not simply within the species of man. It is an ongoing, gigantic opportunity for all things to come into a much grander understanding of themselves. It is the microcosm mirroring the macrocosm. It is one species of planetary beings mirroring their evolutionary journey towards another, showing one another what works and what does not.

Your governments are involved at this time in a tremendously challenging program of their own evolution. Their issues of integrity and their value systems are being challenged to the core of their being. As they have approached these exchanges or meetings with various types of extraterrestrials, most have approached this from a three dimensional point of view rather than realizing that these encounters are multi-dimensional. What we want everyone to understand is that there is always someone behind the scenes operating realities whether you realize it or not.

Some of these extraterrestrials are constructs that are made by others to act as the interceptors between themselves and your reality. Even though some of these extraterrestrials look like living, viable beings fully operative on their own, in fact they are constructs. They are what would be called an interface. They are what one form of consciousness creates in order to meet another where the boundaries are so distant that without an interface there would be no way to interact.

So, many times when you interact with extraterrestrials,

you are not interacting with the primary source. You are interacting on a secondary nature. Many of these extraterrestrial constructs are what your governmentals are working with. It is an interesting thought.

Remember, in speaking to you, it is not so much that we want to define for you your reality as it is, we wish you to expand your definition of it. Never take anything we say literally. Always follow the larger spiral that we are intending to create that allows you to have a bigger picture. Certainly never stop where we put an idea because we are simply there to open up your paradigms. We "rattle your cages" so that you can begin to find the activation of the real knowledge, the true knowledge that is stored inside of you. That is where the data is. The data was stored in great abundance in all living things upon this planet.

Then, because of events as they proceeded, our own planes of existence evolved and we learned about responsibility, integrity, power, etc. There were clashes amongst those who we call your Creator Gods, whose experiment this was. Over many, many millions of years, there were different changes and shifts of administration and the Living Library was changed. In the 1990s, what we are seeing as a result of all of this change over many millennia, is a species that is presently being reactivated by energies from off of your planet. They are carefully electromagnetically, genetically, tooling you, readjusting you. Vibrationally, energies are being beamed to the planet so that the Living Library can once again come into activation.

We said that at one time, when the planet was a battleground, certain energies took over. It is these energies that are what we call your present owners of the planet. Of course, we like to throw out to you that your Earth is a "prime hunk of real estate" and in some world it is owned by someone. There is a collective of energies who believe they own your world. They believe they are stewards for it. They are energies who claim your Earth as their territory, whose flag is planted here. It is an invisible flag. It is a flag that you have not been able to see. *There are owners of your Earth.* Many of your earthly nations have claimed territories which may have belonged to someone else.

As it has been experienced these last 300,000 years or

some such, there has been an ownership on this planet. For their particular reasons they have become quite adept at genetic manipulation. They have rearranged the genetic structure by modulating the frequency at which this planet vibrates. They have changed the amount of information or knowledge available to all of those within the Living Library.

When these energies claimed ownership, they came into territorial management of your globe, and set about a plan, just like anyone who owns and operates something has a plan. The ownership of the planet, as we will tell you the story, came about by a very violent conquest in your terms. There was an immediate need to take the existing species that you would call your representative of man and to formulate an experimentation on this brilliant being that was filled with incredible information. They disassembled the energy connectors, the light encoded filaments, the portion of the living self called the DNA that holds all of this information. There was genetic experimentation, a hybridization practiced between certain energies in different places. They created the disassembling of the DNA structure within the human beings. When this disassembling took place, it was like an unplugging of one's abilities. At that point the brain moved into dormancy.

You have been taught on your planet that you are evolving and that you have not come into full use of the brain and that you have not figured out what it is for. We are saying to you that at one time you were a species that was fully operative with a complete twelve strand DNA helix.

Now, you only have two strands of DNA genetic coding; so, you are no longer fully plugged in. And, thus you cannot access information from the ten inoperable strands. The twelve-stranded program connected each strand to a Living Library of information, a living source center that would feed data through that particular strand of DNA.

It activated the full body potential of the energy occupying the body or human form, the one who took out the library card. Indeed, at one point the body was like a library card. It allowed one to access the library. This DNA was torn apart. Those who took over and understood genetics knew not so much how to *build* something genetically as they knew how to *disassemble* it.

How often on your planet has a conquering force come in and shown their might by tearing down or destroying some monument or building? How often when the raiding lords come in do they build something fantastic? Or do they tear down to show their might? So it was that these raiding lords of energy, these extraterrestrials who claimed ownership and territory of Earth, tore down the existing magnitude and might of the Living Library which was, in fact, the DNA of the human.

Through trial and error and through knowing how to destroy more than knowing how to create, they became the dictators of this place. They set about their plan and they set about their way of giving ideas and data to this land that they owned in order to get this land to produce what they could use for themselves. They took over this incredibly lively place of information. You must realize that Earth was designed to biogenetically store a version of the history of the Universe. This data is stored in the cells of all things here on this planet. The human, when properly tuned and properly plugged in and operable, is the key factor in accessing all of this data. Others come in and merge with the human in order to experience what is here, in order to find data.

We are implying many, many things here. We are asking everyone who reads this to stretch your concepts about who you can be as humans. Those who are in "frequency control" of your planet created a race of slaves; you are taught as a species that you must work to receive. This is a shared paradigm or belief. There are minority cultures, like the aborigines, who are not influenced by the media of your world. These peoples do not have these beliefs because they operate by request, by right of being, or by command.

After the genetic structure was rearranged, it was very easy to control the species as they were only plugged into two of their twelve strands of DNA encoding. Remember everything was still left in the body; it is simply not yet operable.

Now, the story gets very interesting. These raiders of your planet who were biogeneticists to some degree, but certainly not the expert creators the Original Planners were, did not know how to access the Living Library. But they did understand one of the basic tenets of existence, that consciousness is within all things. These clever geneticists, the owners of your planet, decided that the least they could do with all of this wealth was to create a frequency that they could use; therefore they unplugged some of your DNA structure in order to change your vibratory frequency.

They have enticed or directed consciousness to give off a certain vibratory frequency by tricking your consciousness into thinking it has no control of itself. Consciousness that understands that it is self-generating can give off its own signal. When you don't know this, others can trick you into giving off certain signals.

So they created boundaries for you and limitations by coming onto your planet as masters, as teachers, as all kinds of individuals, and setting up concepts of belief, religions, political systems, revolutions, and influencing large masses of consciousness to behave and to vibrate, to give off a certain belief system or frequency.

Belief systems generate feeling. Everyone feels in some way, though they may not know they are in touch with their feelings. All humans are designed to feel to some capacity. When humans are frequency controlled and directed to feel in certain avenues of suppression, which basically is what your planet has been subjected to, they vibrate within a certain range of the electromagnetic spectrum. As there is energy within all consciousness, that energy can be used for whatever one wishes. You do not understand the wealth that is behind the energy of thought or existence. **Other energies do understand and they take that energy. They harvest it from your planet to use for their own needs.**

This is what has been going on for a few hundreds of thousand years now. Of late, there has been a plan orchestrated by the Original Planners to re-establish ownership of your planet because there is something hidden here within the human DNA which the rest of the Universe can benefit from beyond calculation.

The Original Planners have come back to take over your planet by seeding your planet with a force of energies that we have called the Family of Light. Travelling into different systems, they take on the guise of the native system and incarnate or birth themselves. They operate within the system that needs to be altered. This way, those who wish to alter the system from the outside are able to have their agents on the inside, electromagnetically and biogenetically, by careful selection of a blueprint before one enters the human body.

The closest thing you have to understanding your blueprint is your astrological makeup at arrival and, of course, at departure – birth and death. By assisting a massive movement onto the planet within a short amount of time and seeding the Family of Light, the Original Planners plan on changing the evolutionary course of your system.

How do they plan to do this? Those who will be reading this are the ones who are seeded here. You are what we call the Family of Light. You exist to carry information. You are consciousness that has an existence far beyond what you can presently dream about or conceive. You are vast. You are particular in your desire to express yourself within this universal system. Your greatest predilection is to go into frequency controlled systems. You change them by moving incognito, in disguise as the local natives, within a controlled system while receiving bombardments of energy, light, communication, and sound from outside the planet. You then hold these energies into the physical form and agree to go through the process of having the electromagnetic energies reactivate and realign the disassembled DNA.

This is an incredible evolutionary leap for one involved, no matter how much time the process takes. It will take place on an accelerated path for the next twenty years. There are those who have already received a realignment of the twelve strands of DNA, the twelve helixes. These strands of twelve spirals of DNA interact with one another in and outside of the body. With the twelve strands connected, twelve energy or information centers can begin to function and send information back and forth to one another. It is a fiber optic system.

Traditionally, seven of these centers are located in the body. Five of them are located outside of the body. They are aligned with the spinning of the twelve heavenly bodies that you know of at this time within your third dimensional solar system. There are heavenly bodies within your solar system that move in and out of dimensions. We are speaking of the twelve heavenly bodies that are spinning with information, that spin with the chakra systems, that go out to the end of the Universe, and that spin with the DNA spinning inside of the body.

What is happening now is that there is a depth inside of each human that is waiting to be touched. We call these depths codes of consciousness. They are codicils of being. They are what humans are needing eventually to know about themselves. So they are what the Family of Light is beginning to activate within themselves as they play out this part of being in disguise as humans. Those of you who are Family of Light know who you are. You don't feel like you belong here. You feel like you are visiting. You feel as if you are on assignment. We like to say to you that you *are* on assignment, that you have been transported here as systems busters, as keepers of frequency.

Your assignment is to come onto the planet as a human being and then to remember that you are more than human – that you are a greater source of energy. Put it to practical use inside of the human body. As you do this by intention, and as you receive the energies from outside of yourself, everything begins to work because you put it into action.

The greatest concept that has been kept from the planet is the bio-relativity of thought. Yes, what you think, all biological energies, all conscious energies, impact their reality by being. When you direct how you wish to be, you direct the result of what you experience. This is the secret that everyone has done everything to keep the humans from knowing.

When the human DNA begins to activate as a twelve strand helix, and this information begins to be acted upon, there will be incredible power within masses of individuals. Simply by coming together and jointly intending what they want, the individuals become a telepathic receptacle for energies from all over the cosmos.

We want you to understand that as you evolve, you must learn to make choices without dilemmas. Sometimes you do not have choices to make, and even though consciously you do not want to seek out dilemmas – dilemmas create an opportunity to grow. They create opportunities for you to establish your values and to check back and say, "What is important to me? What is it that I stand for? Do I value life? Do I value peace and harmony? Will I commit violence here? What will I condone?"

This is something that every human on the planet is going to confront in these next twenty years. Absolutely! No one will slide under the fence. Everyone, in some way, will encounter a decision with themselves and they will decide what is important to them. This will create a multiplicity of worlds in which one can find oneself because there are many, many worlds and many Earths. As you are taught and as you educate yourselves about your Earth and its evolution, understand that every version of Earth that you can think of is going to exist. Which one do you choose to be on? And, whatever one you choose to be on, do not judge the ones that you are not on because each one creates an arena of opportunity.

Polarities offer an opportunity for great acceleration because you have something from which you can rebound. One of the dualities is called evil. It creates an opportunity for you to reflect its opposite, or what you consider to be its opposite. We will remind you that Prime Creator, the prime source of all energies, is within all things. Even that which you run from, fear most, and believe limits your opportunity, is the Prime Creator.

In actuality, as members of the Family of Light, you are Prime Creator going in to wreak havoc with the Prime Creator's creations. How you wreak havoc as members of the Family of Light is that you create a different frequency by light and by love. We will say to you that the frequency of light is a frequency of information. The frequency of love is the frequency of creation. It is part of what is being reactivated on the planet through the mutating and evolving Family of Light. You will anchor a frequency on the planet which will set the mutation process into activity for the rest of the humans because they have the same genetic structure as you. You simply picked lines of heredity very carefully. You picked lines of genealogy that would best suit your needs and catapult you quickly into higher consciousness. You have to hold a tremendous amount of data and electromagnetic frequency. When you reactivate this, you will bring back to the planet the two basic building blocks which are the foundation of information and creation.

In other words, when the 12 helixes are completely activated, and that takes awhile, they begin to be plugged in. Some of you have experienced having them plugged in. They are not activated now. When they are activated, the full brain is in operation and you become geniuses. You know everything. You become telepathic. You become able to do anything that there is because you are the host of the Living Library. You have "the card" that allows you to access any kind of information that is stored all over this planet. True health, then, would be a completely mutated and evolved twelve helixes inside the body which would activate full brain capacity.

Everything here is stored biogenetically in the DNA and the living structure of all things. Particularly, it is stored in the animal kingdom. Many of the sentient Creator Gods who gathered to do all of this created versions of themselves as living light forms on the planet. Part of their own DNA was put into many of the different species that exist here. Sometimes they are in birds or flowers because they best epitomize the sentient beings' existence.

Returning to this issue of health, we want you to know that you do have power over your body. From infancy you were told that you have no power over your body. The biogeneticists supplied a control paradigm in which you were told that you must always check with someone else about the health and well-being of your body. You have never been told to just say, "Hey, body, how are you doing? Fine? Good, that is what I intend."

You, yourselves, have the innate ability to take charge of your body. You *do* replicate your body daily. You create the same body because you expect to see the same body. If you wish to change it, simply intend that when you wake up there is something new to greet you. You can bring health. You can bring vitality. You can understand that there are many cycles within the body and you can easily live many hundreds of years. You can understand that the body does not age. You expect the body to age and the body ages. You expect the body to deteriorate and you participate in activities that promote the aging and deterioration of the body rather than creating and choosing activities that would promote its rejuvenation.

Health is an area in which everyone needs to claim responsibility for themselves. When responsibility for self is taught and when everyone claims responsibility and stewardship for their own body, health, creations, and appearance – for all aspects of their being – there will be no other education needed. Everything springs from stewardship of the body. **This is true health: accepting complete ownership and responsibility of the magnificent vehicles that you occupy.**

We intend that everyone who reads these words will have an expansion of ideas. We intend that there be forgiveness for all of those who presented you with the limiting ideas under which you and they formerly operated: family members, lovers, friends, associates, teachers or anyone else. There should be forgiveness for yourself and all others who, out of ignorance, instilled limitations. As the individuals are being touched by these words of expansion, by these ideas of limitlessness, your healing thoughts reach out to everyone who ever affected you. So the one who receives our word now becomes the primal teacher broadcasting to everyone you know an unlimited vibration of healing and freedom. And so it is.

We always wish to create the opportunity for greater information, accessibility, operability, effortlessness, fun, prosperity and, sexuality, of course. We cover it all. We don't waste words. We don't waste energy. And, we always have a pocketful of brilliant ideas. When we imprint or interface with your reality, it is our intention that every moment that we are able to affect your reality, we do. We don't just once in awhile use the moments of your reality. **We use every moment that we have in your reality to alter it, to bring it a greater opportunity to understand itself.**

Sometimes we forget that we are speaking to an audience that isn't in the know. From our point of view, you all are in the know. It is just a matter of memory that is stored inside your being though some of you are out there moaning and groaning saying, "We need help and assistance now and again." So let us give you an avenue that you can definitely walk down – a formula that works.

What is that formula? That formula is quite simple. It has to do with you in the moment. It has to do with you every day repeatedly setting out with clarity, the idea of what you wish to experience. Recognize that what you really want may fall into a category of impossibility according to someone else's boundary or limitation. With a sense of righteousness, a sense of deserving and with graciousness identify inside of yourself what it is that will bring you happiness. What is it that makes you feel light and connected and alive to be here? What is it that you desire that will bring you peace on the planet as you occupy your own being? Whatever those things are, begin to want those things. Begin to call those things to yourself by saying, "It is my intention that I experience a harmonious lifestyle. It is my intention that I experience health and energy that leads me to creative adventures. It is my intention that I am well provided for with shelter, food, and all of the things that I need to experience life abundantly. I pass this great abundance on and share it with others."

You were not trained to think of these ideas. Yet, this is how in your greatest use of action you can begin to think this way and then forget about it. Every day devote a small portion of your time, two or three times a day, to getting clear about what you want. Every day open the energy centers in the body and above the body by calling the frequency of light. Picture a beam of light coming into the energy centers outside of the body and the energy centers inside the body. Your chakras are information centers. They are vortexes that, once activated, begin to spin. When they begin to spin they create a movement inside of the body that activates the light-encoded filaments that work together. They rebundle and form the twelve evolving helixes in the body.

We will say also it is very important for everyone who wishes to be in complete balance in their physical body to practice on a regular basis some kind of deep breathing exercise on a regular basis. Practice a program where breathing is important and additional oxygen is brought into the body.

Another recommendation for those who wish to accelerate the activation of their chakras is to spin your body. First check with your body and your spirit as to whether spinning is appropriate for you at this time. Build up to any spinning practice very slowly and always have another person supervise. If appropriate, spin your body from left to right, that is, clockwise, focusing your vision on your extended thumb at eye level while counting. Begin with three to five spins daily over a period of months. Build up to this slowly. It is not that you are going to do it next week. When you complete spinning, however number of times you spin, press your palms together at chest level, keeping the eyes open, and balancing yourself. Place your feet shoulder-width apart, feeling anchored and spinning at the same time. This tremendously accelerates the spinning of the chakra systems inside of the body which increases the rate at which you can receive and interpret data. Is this clear? If you are able to work up to three times a day, spinning ninety-nine times total, well, we will see how long you will stay on the planet, or at least in this dimension.

So, we have given a little bit of instruction on intention, breathing, chakras, and spinning. We will add a post script to that. As electronic beings who are altering their frequency at a very fast rate, we would recommend you drink a tremendous amount of water. Use fresh water, purified water, spring water, or whatever. Water acts as a conduit, a conductor. It keeps the system open and flowing. There are many other things one can do but this will give a start.

Get to know yourselves. You must stop feeling sorry for yourselves. We wish to say that you all have one thing in common. You pity yourselves and hold "pity parties" individually or with others: don't be a victim. Look at all things as an opportunity, no matter how challenging they may seem. You can acknowledge that you feel angry and at the same time say, "Well, I am angry as all get out and at the same time I know that there is some opportunity in this for me."

As members of the Family of Light, you all are going to be challenged to behave in ways that the unevolved or limited DNA humans cannot do. With the DNA coming into full activity, many things that seem impossible will become quite possible. This will unfold for some very quickly. Many will not go public with what they can do because it will take them time to learn their own power. Sometimes you may discover that you can do something quite astounding and you may want to keep it to yourself or to share it only with one or two others.

It is a process of discovering your own wealth. If you were ever to discover how wealthy you were too quickly it could freak you out. This wealth will be uncovered, pooled, and activated within the masses. There will be leadership within the masses who must be able to behave with fairness and honesty, and with great integrity. They must take the resources of this incredible activated energy and use it for the upliftment of all concerned. There are tremendous challenges for honesty, integrity in the use of power in the years that are coming. Tremendous powers are going to be unleashed, first within the Family of Light.

We will remind you that just as the Original Planners are able to employ and insert the Family of Light into their old project to assist them in regaining territorial ownership, other forces are able to do quite the same. There is a polarity going on at this time – a plan. There are many plans within plans.

There are other energies who have evolved over these last few hundred thousand years who are creating their own genetic line for the purpose of suppressing the planet. Those off-planet energies have their on-planet operatives. Sometimes the on-planet operatives do not know that they are run by someone else, although now many do.

This is where you need the multidimensional self, the multispecied self, for as you will come to very quickly find out, intelligent forms occupy a variety of molecular combinations. You will find that many species are in combination with what you call animal kingdom and what would be called human. Interesting, is it not?

We wish to present these ideas to our readers so they may embrace what they are hesitant about or fearful of. When you face these so-called dark, shadowy portions of yourself, you create an opportunity of liberation for all. Because the final and first tenet is: *thought creates*. No matter what situation you find yourself in, within it is the power of thought. The underlying and impeccable belief that brings you back to your power of thought is that it will create the transformation of your experience and the planetary existence. Understood?

Your species cannot be aware at this time of the cosmic rhythms and cycles that influence you. First, you do not agree that there is life outside the planet. The mass consciousness at this time does not believe that there is a higher intelligence cycle. Of course there is. We will speak about it from an intellectual point of view and we will trust that within the next few years this will become experiential for the planet. You will gain an experiential knowing that you are part of a tremendous cycle.

There are cycles of ownership. There are cycles of stewardship. There are cycles of summer and winter and spring and fall. Consciousness moves in the same way. There are cycles of what you call good and cycles of what you may call evil. You are coming to an end of a cycle where forces have been orchestrating their plans for a long time to create an incredible opportunity for all involved. No one is a loser. There are no losers ever. There are only opportunities for consciousness to play itself out.

When an actor plays the part of the villain in a drama, is he a loser for playing that part? He gets compensated for playing that part, does he not? He may be the star of the show and be compensated more than anyone else. He creates a drama, an opportunity around which every other consciousness plays. Please be aware that as polarities begin to magnify themselves that there is, indeed, a purpose to it. Don't be frightened about which of the energies are revealing their plans and purposes upon your planet because there is no one plan. There are plans within plans as there are cycles within cycles.

We said at one time that your Universe is part of a cycle that makes up a number of other universes: twelve. We said also that just as a hundred pennies equal a dollar, a hundred universes must equal something else. Do you understand? There are different ways of collecting energy together and forming what would be called different approaches to consciousness, different approaches to existence.

As a species, you are approaching the end cycle. It is coming about in the next twenty years and has been called by some, by those who have this belief system, the end of times. Indeed, it is an ending. It is an incredible ending. Always when there is an ending there is a beginning because nothing ever terminates. All things continuously move on, even when consciousness is destroyed. There is consciousness within all things. So even in its destruction does it create an opportunity to amass itself in the new version. Do you follow the paradox of all of this?

The peak cycle that the Earth is coming to is a cycle that has the ability to bring about incredible change. Whenever there is an opportunity for incredible change, many, many energies will gather for the sake of being there; simply to experience being in the vicinity of change. The nature of this change, including the gigantic step-up in electromagnetic frequency that is planned to occur on this planet (or a version of this planet), is magnetically drawing back all previously involved energies to participate in the liberation of the control of humans.

Liberation, indeed, is one of the plans that will come about. Which plan will you find yourself in? Which world or which reality will you create by belief? Which one will be yours? Which one are you coded to respond to? Do you feel powerless in what you are coded to respond to?

If something is firing your codings and you do not like it, simply state very clearly that you are not available for that program and that you wish to be taught or accelerated or activated in a different way; this is quite important. Sometimes when you were making your DNA blueprints, you also made certain plans. However, when your plans did not live up to your expectations, you could change them. You can always change to receive data and experience in a different way. You are never powerless.

Let us say something about the cycles here. We said that we are speaking to the Family of Light and that they are on assignment here on Planet Earth. You members of the Family of Light are also on assignment simultaneously in other controlled systems of existence. There the frequency, the electromagnetic structure within which the existing species operates, is controlled. These other systems are presently evolving in a similar fashion. It does not mean that they are like Earth; it means they are undergoing a similar drama. However, it is not possible for them to gather as much informational experience as they want.

So, the cycles of existence are becoming more powerful because of what happens as more electromagnetic energy is able to be housed in one specific branch of multidimensional self. As you become aware of your multidimensional existence, you begin to recircuit your conscious self, not just your physical self, by sending the energy from one multidimensional energy to another.

In this way you begin to understand the evolved being that the twelve helixes represent. What the twelve helixes of the expanded DNA show the human is that they exist in many places at many times.

Allowing other aspects of your multidimensional self to come through you and access information is part of being a Living Library card. It is an interdimensional cinematographic experience of your many selves.

You Family of Light members holding these human bodies, have human nervous systems that are very rapidly evolving to accommodate all of these incoming signals. Eventually you will be able to translate them. These signals are not being blasted full force onto the planet at this time because this would blow the planet up. There is a steady increase of energy.

As the Family of Light members are able to receive, hold and anchor the evolving energy, it becomes *here*. More information comes through on this electromagnetic wave as the magnetic frequency is increased. You, then, act as radios by becoming living energy, and broadcasting it out to others without a word – simply by being keepers of the frequency that you know is your higher identity.

If there is anything to which our audience can aspire, we would ask you all to become impeccable keepers of frequency. That means keeping knowledge and information of the highest order inside of yourself. You make that frequency available for all around you by simply living it – walking your streets, shopping in your stores, simply resting on your pillow in the evening, and knowing who you are.

Let us speak for a moment here about heredity. There is a magnificence to the plan that makes up your blueprint of your genetic structure. Each human being who is born selects the genetic makeup that best suits the impression that they wish to make in that reality, the experience that they wish to gather for themselves.

As members of the Family of Light, a great effort was expended and great diligence was put forth to coalesce genetic lines within the breeding program of Earth.

Part of this breeding program has given you accessibility for more rapid evolution. In other words, those members of the Family of Light who feel you are not human and wonder why you are on Earth, have selected genealogical lines where the recessive qualities in both parents were available to be genetically mixed together. It is within the *recessive gene* that the opportunity to come into full operation and activity is held. Genetics and your hereditary line are all very important parts of your coming into reality.

Your genetic blueprint is coordinated with the exact moment and the exact geographical, astrophysiological data of your birth that gives you your impetus to be. Your astrological reading charts are the vestige of what you have left to interpret who you chose to be in this lifetime. Your chart is a good opportunity to begin your interpretation of who you are; although, it is much more complex than this.

Heredity is self-chosen. All of the cosmos works to influence you. Whatever system you live within, all of the physical and non-physical planetary bodies around it operate to influence your choices, your motivations, your experiences.

Soon will come the interdimensional planets that are within the solar system. This may not occur until much later on when your scientists realize that there is another solar system that operates on another dimensional frequency. If there is incredible advancement in the minds and integrity of the scientists, those who operate with love will far surpass the technological advancements previously kept secret from them.

When individuals and groups operate with the vibration of love and creativity, coupled with the vibration of light and wisdom, then there will be an incredible flood of knowledge and remembering onto this planet.

All things, all possibilities will exist.

Chapter 12

Tianna, Dr. Socree
& Korton

Channeled by Mark Niclas

Tianna last incarnated on Earth some 45 years ago, and was the physical sister to the channel, Mark Niclas, before her death. She now resides on her home planet of Shacare within the Pleiadian star system.

Greeting in the Light to Be. This is Tianna.

I am asked to speak to you in regards to the importance of your genetic code/pattern of life which you call the DNA, and the transformations that are presently taking place within it. I believe it is useful to understand how the DNA was formed without getting too scientific/medical, so please let me take you on a journey that will get you thinking. As Brother Sananda says, "Think to remember – don't remember to think."

Perhaps you know the Earth is being bathed with great amounts of vibrational healing rays. As these rays go to work with all living things upon and within your planet, many wondrous happenings take place. For those of you who are going through constant weight gain and loss – sugar cravings – sleep disorders and even brief periods of skin breakout – don't panic. These and many other occurrences are a part of the great changes taking place within all of the inhabitants on Mother Earth – also called Akasha, Gaia and the Emerald Planet.

Let's go back billions of years to the planet Earth as it

begins to cool down from its birth. If we were to journey back in time we would be very aware of the smells, the sounds and the sensations...the smells of burning sulphur...the sounds of hissing gases and the electrical sensations of a newborn entity filled with excitement. Your planet, Gaia, was just initiated into the universal realm of planets. She was impregnated with many cosmic patterns and energies. Mother Earth has also been seeded with a special ingredient for producing life forms. The fusion of electromagnetic and organic particles of light, spinning wildly into vortexes of energy, will eventually give birth to the first microorganism. It is here that I wish to venture with you. Have you for any moment in your life contemplated what components constitute the electromagnetic/biological makeup of your bodies?

Your physical bodies are composed of the same components which make up your earth. Your scientists can spend hundreds of hours and trillions of dollars trying to capture the true meaning of life but they will always miss this one important point. The very essence of your makeup lies in the same genetic mold that has caused your earth to form volcanoes, create oceans and even stay in balance through gravity.

As the Earth began to cool down and the particles of dust began to settle, an amazing concoction began to take shape. The mingling of electromagnetic/biological and foreign (extraterrestrial) debris began to seep slowly into the soft spongy wet surface of the new Mother Earth. The highly charged brew of newly married life source components caused the first bank of steam to rise towards the sky as it danced together with the molten hot magma that was seeping up through the cracks of the Earth's face.

Picture this: the inner Earth's blood, lava – its Life Force comes into contact with virgin essences that will eventually, over millions of years, spring forth Life Spirit. What happens when powdered incense is sprinkled over hot glowing charcoal? Imagine the smoke is steam – the charcoal is the lava and finally the beautiful smells are the new Life Spirit. Can you also see the overlay – the mirror image for the DNA – as it was seeded by the twisting together of the Gold and Silver Rays? They assisted in the creation of this planet, by coming together and forming it from the inside out.

Over time, the steam rose and collected itself in banks (clouds). With the constant pressure of gravity and the steady flow of radioactive waves of Light, the first rains started. Now this is where I need to venture off and add some things that are galactic in nature.

There were many watching this birth from distant star systems and galaxies. They had known of this birth and were waiting with excitement for the time when they would see the new star's light shine. Teams of scientists were sent out from various star systems to observe and even assist in the birth. Since the other star systems were far advanced in their sciences of working with the elements of nature, they were able to produce and offer essences of life-breathing nectars from their various homes. As the rains began to pour down upon the cooling new planet the scientists, who were implored to add assistance, went to work.

Have you ever wondered where some creations came from? Some animals, plant species and mineral compositions that your scientists cannot figure out? Well, the ones from the distant stars added their own unique alchemies to the Earth.

Through releasing specific gases common in their land, these spacefaring Light Workers assisted the Earth in her mission to breathe forth Life Spirit. High doses of Xenon, Argon, Crypton and Magnon (a gas not known now on your planet, but its mutant change cousin called Monoxide is) were released into the primitive, not yet developed atmosphere. The Doctors of Light were only able to stay around for this brief yet delicate transformation. For then the greatest occurrences began to happen. Now that the cosmic ingredients were added to the brew of earthean organic matter, a great soup began to form the earth's oceans.

The oceans took many years to form during which mass movements of the Earth's surface began to be remolded. With the enormous volcanic eruptions and the highly volatile explosions caused by the fusion of the organic and foreign gases, your planet went into millions of years of growth, change and transformations. This event had never been seen anywhere before. It was obvious to the Space People that something extraordinary was being put together across the blue black sea of night.

Before we leave that time space, let me add this thought. The fragments of energy that comprise your spiritual and etheric bodies are extraterrestrial in nature. Extraterrestrial simply means existing beyond Earth's surface. The Earth is a baby. The *guests* of Earth are ancient.

As we speak now about the formation of the DNA, you will see what I mean when I say that every living energy from the smallest cell to the largest mammal was seeded with spiritual knowledge from the vast cosmos – the heart space of God/Goddess or the Mother/Father realms.

When Gaia danced and sang, her body contorted into rhythmic movements, her blood pouring freely from her womb. A beautiful sound began to be heard by her Spirit. Gaia was about to be awakened. Since she was the newest creation in the sea of stars, it was time for her baby shower.

I am often times told about this event and it gives me pleasure to speak about it. I hope that when you, my brothers and sisters of planet Earth, read this, you, also, will be able to know and feel the healing power in *sound*.

A call was placed to all members of the Planetary Council of Light, asking them to send the new star the sound that would awaken the Spirit and deliver the soul of Gaia – the Earth Mother. The sound was the OM. For a period equivalent to seven Earth days, those upon the Pleiades and the other members of the council sang from their hearts the radiant healing tone of OM. I am told you could actually see the sound as it collected together to form what is termed to you an aura. This silvery white material, with magnificent colors throughout its mass, made its way towards the Earth planet. As you know, the sound of the OM is the universal sound that comes from the very vibration of the Creator's heart. When the sound reached the outer atmosphere of your Earth it surrounded your planet, creating its own auric band of protection.

Your planet was now ready to begin its long-awaited chain of events to produce the Tree of Life. I am reminded to mention that which you call the Northern Lights are descendants of the original light show formulated from the choir of OMs.

Now that Earth was properly sealed with protection, the Life Forces began their spiraling ascension. There are many books you can read about the chain of events that brought about the (human) body that is enabling you to hold this book, so I shall skip quickly through the millions of years stopping at strategic points along evolution's path.

Lightning and ultraviolet light from the sun were breaking apart simple hydrogen-rich molecules in the primitive atmosphere. Fragments of these molecules were spontaneously recombined into more complex molecules. In the meantime, remember, the oceans had already formed and were quite fertile. The products of the chemistry with the complex molecules began to form in the oceans, causing new and unique strands of life-bearing possibilities. A kind of cosmic soup of gradually increasing complexity began to mix together with the cosmic ingredients that were already stirred into the pot.

Many, many years became the spoon which stirred the soup, until one day quite by accident – or was it an accident? – a molecule came into being that was able to produce copies of itself using, as building blocks, the other molecules in the soup. This was the ancestor of the DNA. The DNA is known as the master molecule of life on Earth!

Again, you can read many reports on the components of DNA, but do keep in mind the spiritual side of the DNA – the energy that was the food or matrix from which DNA was created. Those spices, cosmic ingredients, came from the Creator's own garden. These spices of life are the key to using the techniques to be given later by my co-workers in this project.

For if the mighty DNA did not have any spiritual qualities it would not have been able to perform the magical alchemy of copying itself to form one of the first clones, or shall I say the first Higher Self and ego?

It is from this step here that many of life's incredible mysteries stem. For example, how did Cain and Abel, Adam and Eve's male children, produce offspring? Was it that they utilized the magical spices found in the DNA to produce from their own essence a copy of themselves? How does a chameleon grow back its own tail after it is pulled off? What is this concept of cloning? You will see many of life's mysteries start to tell their true stories in times to come.

Some 4.5 billion years ago, the ancestors of the DNA molecule were competing for building blocks on which to grow. The spice of life was everywhere. The stuff things are made of was plentiful. Many of you who have heard me speak through my brother, Mark, are familiar with the term I coined – "mutant change."

As I have repeatedly said, a mutant change does not mean that one will change into a hideous monster with strange appendages. Rather, it is one of the most, if not *the* most, powerful transformational alchemies to ever take place. It is the event that takes place through the birthing of new opportunities for change in the life of a living thing. Right now your own DNA cellular structure is going through a mutant change.

But this is nothing new, for billions of years ago, the mutant change began when the programming of the directions for the four major levels of the DNA reproduction, known as the nucleotide, "misspelled" their pattern equation.

Each set of instructions that is spelled out is different for each organism. This not only tells you why each organism (any living being, plant or animal) is unique unto itself, but it explains beautifully how different species are born. Without a mutant change, without this divine mistake of nature, everything would look alike. Let's contemplate how the mutant change worked with creating the marvels of Mother Nature.

Eventually plants, fish and the like came out of the water to breathe. Through many stages and millions of years of time, coupled with the magic of mutant change and the DNA molecules exploration of possibilities to create new organisms, the reptiles were born. Then came the amphibians, the dinosaurs, the mammals and the birds. Life was crawling, swimming, flying and walking all over the face of the proud new Mother, Gaia. This new chapter of life, as unique as it was, was not the final act.

All of a sudden, after some 160 million years of dominating the Earth's surface, the dinosaurs perished. Some of my elders say that at first they were gentle to their new home, working and walking peacefully as if they were gently massaging the face of the Earth. As the years passed on and they became frustrated with their lives, great fights began to take place. Some say that their spiritual nature was feeling the mutant change beginning to once again sweep through the organisms of all life on Earth and they knew it would soon be time to leave.

The dinosaurs' cellular/immune system began to diminish as ego took over and their reign of superiority was slackened with the onslaught of Earth changes. Thus one chapter of life, as composed through the DNA, was ended.

Is it not safe to say that the Earth and its inhabitants are going through similar experiences now, with the exception of the cellular/immune system that will not diminish, but will transform.

Thank you for our time together. I now give this next section to Dr. Socree of the White Star.

Dr. Socree last incarnated in Atlantis to assist in the balancing of the Earth and her peoples by administering alchemical energies into the airwaves in order to stabilize the vibrational fields around the planet. He now works as a crew team member on the White Star, once known as the Star of Bethlehem, in the role of an alchemical healer.

DR. SOCREE: Salutations. Yes, it is true one chapter of the book of Akashic records ended and the dinosaurs perished, but as you quickly turn the pages to the next chapter, another event started. The Earth began preparing herself for the greatest event in her history. There was much to do and no time to spare.

The first Ice Age came quickly, sweeping the lands with frigid temperatures that were as healing to the Earth as they were detrimental to her guests. The Ice Age was used to enact a newly seeded remembrance that the Spirit of the Earth had agreed to house a new species of Beings. These Beings were to be initiated into a schoolhouse of life and the final test upon graduation would be the remembrance that they were created in the image of that which created them: God. Much preparatory work was at hand. Even though

Tianna did not cover this in her story, I am sure you are aware that the Earth had been visited in its initial stages by the Elohim race - which seeded the planet with its Akashic records. (This is written about in the book entitled <u>Ancient Lands</u>, Dove Center, 1990.)

During the Ice Age, the DNA cellular structure of the Earth was quickened to high vibratory rates in order to slow her heart beat down to withstand the power and energy about to be unleashed upon her again. There have been at least four major glaciations known as Ice Ages. Each one has prepared the Earth for the next set of visitors.

The most recent Ice Age began about 125,000 years ago and reached its maximum coverage approximately 18,000 years ago. All of eastern Canada was covered by a single frozen mantle. Glaciers in the western mountains had fused together and merged with the Canadian sheet to form a continuous expanse of ice that reached from coast to coast.

Your planet can still be considered to be in the Great Ice Age, although in something of an intermission. Large portions of the Earth's crust such as Greenland and Antarctica still remain covered in ice. "The Great Ice Age" coincided with the rise of humans to prominence on the planet.

It has only been two million years ago that the human type species came on the scene. Remember, this planet has housed at least four separate civilizations coming from the many dimensions. Now you might wonder about when the Atlantean and Lemurian civilizations began and where they fit in.

Ever since the first race of humanity came into being, there were star-seeded codings of life impregnated into them. These Beings are considered to be Earthean in nature though they exemplified what is now termed the fourth dimensional qualities of life. The cave people of primitive days were more evolved than you might want to believe. I remember visiting with them many times. Your ancestory is very special. So are you.

Now that we have given you a brief overview of the DNA and your Earth, let us take a look at the great change that is currently happening upon your planet. How can you prepare for it? How can you assist your physical body in healing itself during these times?

Many changes are taking place within those that are conscious of their Godhood. Once again your home base is going through a major catharsis. This time the dimensions are transforming and along with this the consciousnesses are being heightened to new awareness. You have no doubt heard of the idea of moving into the fourth dimension. Presently you are living with a three-way mirror reflecting the images of God through Mother (female) and Father (male). This is also called the Trinity.

As you move into the fourth dimension a new reflection opens up – the one of Self. Self or I Am, God/Goddess reflecting through Mother/Father back unto Self. Do you get my point? The final stage towards walking in the enlightenment of divinity is when you can see God in your own image. This is what the fourth dimension is all about; it is the next step in reclaiming your divinity.

I do not wish to put a damper on some of the New Age ideologies that say the fourth dimension is just about interdimensional travel, psychic gifts and living in light bodies. The fourth dimension is much broader than that.

Yes, you can utilize these talents if you desire, but you will not always find the need for them since you will be living in the realm that Brother Sananda calls "Think – Create – Manifest."

In the fourth dimension, you will have the ability to be very aware of all things. The most important gift that you will remember is the gift of healing. Healing requires being in touch with all the mirrors of life presented to you when you were only able to view things three dimensionally before.

In the third dimension you cannot generally see the full divinity. In the fourth dimension all aspects of the mirror are presented. The feminine intuitive side, the masculine intellectual side and the divine side, wherein you pull it together and heal it all through love.

One of the keys to moving into this next stage of evolution is through utilizing healing techniques that will assist you in remembering the divinity that you are. Tools of love and techniques of putting into practice that love is the greatest medicine, as when Jesus/Sananda healed.

He pulled strength from his love for the Mother/Father realms, the love for the person he was healing, the love of the universe and the love for his own God-Self. He used the fourth dimension healing techniques.

HEALING YOURSELF

Your physical bodies are coded at a carbon-based rating of 6-6-6. This means that the chemical properties of your organic matter correlate to that specific vibronic rate.

As your DNA cellular structure goes through its mutant change, the body begins to speed up not only its vibrational metabolism, but also its capability of handling higher frequencies of growth change. Thus, your body's cellular structure is slowly changing to a 9-9-9 or diamond-based body.

This is where the concept of a light body comes in. Many exciting things happen within your physical body! First of all, the cells are beginning to expand, not in physical proportion, but through interdimensional transmutation. In order to allow for the higher frequencies of light to move through your Beingness, your cells need space to house these new light vibrations.

This may answer why many of you are constantly finding yourself going through little episodes of what you term illnesses. Actually some of these episodes are very healthy for you. If you were to look at them in a new light, you would greatly assist them in the cleansing taking place.

Take, for example, your common cold. Your body is practicing balancing temperatures, because your Mother Earth has a direct influence on your physical bodies. The very idea that the Earth is drastically shifting her seasons, due to the pollution and other substances that cause her own illness, should assist you in seeing how your body is preparing for the coming times.

A simple direct-link dedication similar to the way Native Americans work with the Earth's Spirit will greatly reduce your risk of catching a cold. Consciously working with the changes both on a physical level and a spiritual level will do wonders.

Each time your physical body goes through some form

of illness or dis-ease, it is trying to tell you something. Wake up, become aware, get on line! Dis-ease indicates a discordance with a natural way of things.

Humankind is now going through a major house cleaning. Your cells are doing whatever they can to accommodate the large amount of high frequencies that are being directed into the Earth. Cancer, AIDS and even birth defects are a direct-link connection to that which is being done to the very body of the Earth you live upon.

If positive natural ways of life do not come into practice on a daily basis, you can expect to see your physical body react in detrimental ways. You will also see your hostess – Gaia – react. Disease, pollution, illness, earthquakes, death, even the shifting of the axis. It all fits. I return you now to Tianna. Peace be to you! Dr. Socree.

Tianna speaking once again. Greetings in the Light.

The following information is based upon our understanding of sound with exercises and techniques that can be applied to healing.

SOUND

The use of sound dates back to the very beginning of creation. Have you ever heard the sound of the Creator's thoughts? Close your eyes for a moment and listen. What do you hear? Were there many thoughts running inside your head? We call this chatter.

Calming the chatter is probably the most important tool in your healing.

Your thoughts, many of which are programmed from society, are said to contain the elements that cause many of your illnesses. For example, when it's cold and rainy outside, and you're walking to work with no umbrella and no rain gear, what would your thoughts be? Most people would be thinking, "Oh, I am going to be sick; I'll catch my death of cold!"

Suppose your boss fired you from your job **and** when you got home, you found a letter saying your car payment was late. Do you start going into stress? Do your muscles get tense? Is there a headache coming on?

Would you reach for a stiff drink...or would you sit right down in a comfy seat and utilize a healing technique? Many of you would do something other than heal yourselves. This is not your fault. You have been programmed this way, through commercials, through societal and family input and through peer pressure. Let's look at how sound could help greatly in these and other circumstances.

As we have said, the Earthean body of a human and the Earth body of Gaia are made from the same components of life. The Earth Mother has a crystalline grid structure running through her. The Earthean body, too, has a grid structure composed of chakras, meridians and energy ley lines.

If you could (and some of you can) hear the sound of the Earth, you would hear a vibrational sound similar to the OM. At times it is very low, and at times extremely high. The Earth is using this sound to balance everything from its poles to the negative/positive polarities that make up the energy for gravity. You can use this same technique for healing and calming your body.

USING SOUND FOR HEALING

Sit in a comfortable position in your favorite place. Close your eyes and place an extra bubble of light protection around you. Pulling down an extra light bubble around you is a good idea, but don't think you are not safe if you forget.

Call to your Higher Self and your friends of the Light for assistance. Ask them to come play and have fun with you as you heal the energy fields around and within you. This is light work. Lighten the load by having fun.

Place your left hand (receiving) over your heart space and your right hand (giving) over your solar plexus. Allow your breathing to gently calm down to the point where you are very comfortable yet very alert. Then, offer up a prayer.

I give this prayer to you as an example:

Dear Mother/Father God – Creator of All that Is – I come to you to ask for assistance in healing myself with your love. I call upon the angels of transmutation and healing to be with me. *So be it. It is done.*

Rest in these energies for a while. You may begin to feel

electrical impulses coming through your hands and running throughout your body. This is good as it will charge your cellular structure with healing rays. After you are comfortable and much of the chatter in your mind has rested, begin to sound the OM as low as possible. Sound the OM as long as you can and eventually bring the sound to be continuous, taking a breath only when needed. The sound should resonate in your solar plexus.

If there are thoughts that are needing to be loved away, that have been causing you discomfort, send these thoughts through the OMs and ask that the angels of transmutation take them back to the universal pool of thoughts fully cleansed.

If you need healing, concentrate on that specific area while OMing in these low tones. Allow all emotions and feelings to come up. Release to the light all the frustrations, discomfort or illness that is afflicting you.

When you are ready to move to the next step, discontinue sounding the OM and just breathe gently for a few minutes. Check your mental chatter again. If there is still chatter either go back to sounding the low OMs or just continue breathing until you are comfortable. When ready sound the OM in your normal voice range.

As you do this allow your thoughts the freedom to play with you and show you beautiful things about yourself and your life. Once again, sound the OM with only a short breath in between.

When you are ready to move to the next step, discontinue sounding the OM and just breathe gently for a few minutes. The final step is to sound the OM at the highest range possible for your particular voice.

As you are doing this, send thoughts of positive movement and direction throughout your body and into the universe. After you are comfortable and feel aligned, rest for a few moments, breathing gently.

This is a good time to move into a meditation. If there is a mirror nearby, go to it and look at your reflection and say: "I love all that you are." **Smile**. Thank the Spirit energies around you and enjoy. This exercise may be done in pairs or in groups.

WHAT ARE YOU CONNECTING TO WITH THE SOUNDS?

OMing in low sound connects you to the inner Earthean realms. You are not only assisting your body in grounding itself, you are sending much needed energy to the Earth. OMing in normal voice range opens your energy field to connect with the natural flow of life as it runs through all living beings. OMing in a high voice connects you into the universal flow and gives the DNA cellular structure some added juice by creating an electromagnetic field (through sound). Most cells sing at extremely high field vibration.

The use of a gong or other low vibration instrument is very useful when OMing in the low range. The gong is used by many of the Inner-Earthean Beings during their healing ceremonies.

The sound of the *low* OM and the gong calls attention to the cellular structure by opening a doorway to them through the vibration. The use of Tibetan bells or cymbals during the *high* OMs greatly assists the cellular structure by giving the body vibratory healing through its pitch.

Most Tibetan bells contain silver in the cymbals which produce a beautiful pitch. The silver also contains specific vibratory healing qualities.

Now it is time to depart and welcome Korton. May the Source be with you. Tianna

Korton is responsible for communication responses with the Universal Brotherhood of Light. He is also a member of the crew team with the White Star.

Blessings to you. This is Korton. At this time I wish to bring information about integration energies for vibrational healing and introduce a very special and unique healing technique not previously known to earth, called the Brain Quadrant Healing Technique.

First, I will explain how to integrate the four quadrants or sectors of your brain. Then I will give you an integration technique to balance yourself within your own field of energy, so that you can heal yourself, others and Mother Earth.

QUADRANT HEALING

Let us first talk about your head area. From a top view, divide your head into four equal parts or sections. Two of these on each side of an imaginary center line. *(See diagram)*

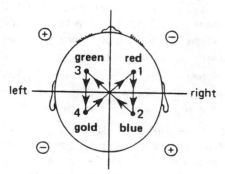

view from the top of the head

If you simply divide your head into four equal parts or quadrants, realize that each quadrant is either negative or positive. Two quadrants are negative and two are positive, much like a battery. They co-balance each other in polarity.

This helps the electromagnetic frequencies that come into balance and integrate mental, physical, emotional, etheric and the other subtle bodies that are around your auric field. Does this make some sense to you?

Looking down onto the top of the head, again, notice there are four small circles outside the head itself. Two of these have - minus signs inside the circle and two have a + inside the circle. The - sign we will call <u>NEGATIVE</u>, meaning HOT energy and the + sign means <u>POSITIVE</u>, or COLD energy.

Now look at the four brain quadrants and see which two quadrants are negative and which two are positive. Your positive brain quadrants <u>receive</u> energy and the negative ones <u>send</u> energy out (giving).

REMEMBER: The "-" is Negative = HOT = giving out. The "+" is Positive = COLD = receiving in.

201

The "+" is Positive = COLD = receiving in.

Neither is good or bad; both are needed. They co-balance each other in polarity. Notice the arrows starting in the top right quadrant with the color red. Follow that down to blue, up and over to the top left, green, down to gold and then back to red. This is like an infinity eight being activated within your brain. Most human brains have only about 5 per cent of their possible capabilities awakened at this time.

Think of it! Those you call genuises may have slightly more access to universal knowing, but earth's population is very much asleep. A massive shift is occurring, however, and you will see many exciting changes!

You also have polarity in your feet, using the same colors. Yes, the negative factor is on your right small toes and the right portion of the heel is positive. Right big toe is positive, and the left portion of the heel is negative. On the left foot - the same thing. *(See diagram)*

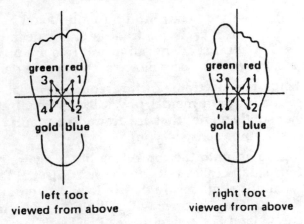

left foot
viewed from above

right foot
viewed from above

These four colors, along with white or silver (a universal "basic" color), are the main colors being sent to you by the communicator ships, or the starships, that you see in your night skies. These starships are also assisting in the healing and the activation of your "light bodies."

Light bodies are a term we use for the development and refrequency attunements happening to your physical bodies through the DNA changes. Eventually the human body will become lighter in its density and free of all dis-eases and imbalances by being "at-one-ment" with the light frequencies of the universal realms.

If you want to do a healing energy to balance your polarity, to assist in the reprogramming of the DNA in your cellular structure, you would simply activate the quadrant sectors in your *head* and *feet*, creating a vortex of energy between them. Some call that a vacuum. The healing energy would go in so that you get both of these energies vibrating inside of your physical body. Put quite simply, you activate the two fields in your brain and feet simultaneously.

You also can take an energy and shoot it out from the base of your feet into the center of the earth for grounding, and you can also send that same energy from the top of your head into the Universe. (This is for your discretion and choice.)

EXERCISE FOR HEALING YOURSELF

Call in your guardian lights for protection. Also call on your fourth dimensional guides. They are the guides who have been watching over you during your awakening transition into the higher frequencies. If you need a guide's name, ask! However, just allowing this Being to exist around you with love is, in my opinion, the best way.

Touch the right front top of your head, or imagine the first sector, and think "RED." You can just literally see a red light going off. Don't do it too fast. Take the time to think and see the red quadrant. *(See head diagram if needed.)*

Touch or imagine the right rear sector and think "BLUE." Touch or imagine the left front sector and think "GREEN." Touch or imagine the left rear sector and think "GOLD." Repeat at least three times. You have now activated all four colors, and they are turning on what I would call beams of energy.

You have now allowed the vortexes of energy to come into your brain and also allowed them to come up from your feet. When you activate your head, your feet will also be activated.

This is total fourth and fifth dimensional energy, working with etherics and your head may vibrate, so <u>take it easy</u>.

Be assured that after you are done with this work, whether you fall asleep or not, it will shut itself off. It is programmed just as some of your computers are programmed. After a certain time of not being used, it will go off. Mind you, you are initiating the action and then your guides take over. This is why so many times you fall asleep while meditating or get so spaced-out you don't know what's going on.

Once you have your healing going on, you can send healing energy down to the core of the earth, or out in the universe, or use it for yourself and others. If you want to heal your own cellular structure, you just allow the vortex of this vacuum to work within your body.

If there are certain things that you want to heal, whether it's a cancer, AIDS, a tumor, skin problems or anything else, program it by sending a thought, just as you would feed information into a computer chip.

This is actually what fourth and fifth dimensions are all about. It's very automatic, in a way. They involve your thought process. This is why in third dimension, going into fourth, we ask you to work on your entire thought process and clean it up.

What you think, you will have.

Program only positive thoughts when activating this energy or rest assured you will be sick. If you positively program for healing, you will be healed. It's that simple!

Now that you have activated the brain quadrant color series, please complete the following visualization before doing the integrating exercises. Create in your mind a little balancing scale with an arrow which can move to the positive (cool) side, the negative (hot) side or remain balanced in the center.

To balance your own physical energies, simply visualize the needle going to dead center. You may feel an energy running through you, or sense that you are more centered and balanced.

INTEGRATING EXERCISES

All right, let us say that you are here at the center of the balancing scale. Now you are ready to integrate your many energy fields.

1. INTEGRATION FOR THE PHYSICAL BODY

You cross your palms over your heart. The sound or tonal that we will use is the OM. You sing this tonal OM at least three times in a row. What you should feel is a vibration that runs from your mouth all through your body. The idea is to produce a vibration that you can feel running through you. It is important, because the tonal OM assists in the energy.

The activation is done like this: A tonal OM out, followed by a free breath (inhaling + exhaling, without OMing.) Repeat two more times.

2. INTEGRATION FOR THE MENTAL/EMOTIONAL BODIES

In this case, you apply the palms of your hands on your temples, and you simply allow your fingers to rest on top of your head. Again, you repeat the activation as explained above: Tonal OM, free breath; tonal OM, free breath; tonal OM, free breath.

3. INTEGRATION FOR THE ETHERIC BODY

While sitting on a chair, raise your left arm at the elbow, palm facing away from you, as in waving. Your right arm rests on your right thigh, palm facing down.

You can raise your right forearm slightly off your thigh, palm facing down, for it will feel right to keep it that way.

Again, practice the tonal OM and free breath three times as explained above.

We recommend caution in doing these exercises too fast or too frequently, especially in the beginning when you are a novice. Working in pairs and groups early on is the best practice.

Energy is very real although you cannot see it, so as you make a deeper study and use of it, respect it and experiment judiciously. Our realms and your guides are assisting you and desire only your safety and happiness.

Nonetheless, each of you is responsible for your energy decision and action. Through this, you achieve mastery and establish future probabilities for yourself, the human family, your planet, solar system and galaxy.

STAR CHAKRA

The Star Chakra embodies itself approximately three to four inches above the Crown Chakra, and contains the genetic make-up of your lives, otherwise known as the Akashic Records.

The Star (or eighth) Chakra works entirely in the Etheric Body. This is the body that connects to the psychic and auric fields that make up the specific energy coding of the Human Being.

One last thing: as you use the exercises for self-healing, you will notice the importance of Higher Self connection and trust. The awareness of the Star Chakra will enable you to be "on-line" with your communication from this source, just as your energy and state of mind will expand to encompass the wholeness of your Being, even the aspects that are not physically perceivable. Then you will be balanced for greater cosmic communication and, perhaps, telepathy.

Remember, many things are not yet perceivable in the human mind. Spirit has in store, for those who seek, many mansions filled with wondrous things.

QUADRANT HEALING OF THE FEET - EXPLANATION BY MARK NICLAS

In the healing process of the feet, there has been some confusion. Originally, the exercise was explained to me that you need only to bring the negative/positive polarities into your feet by separating the right and the left foot. Applying a negative charge to the right set of toes (including big toe) and the positive charge to the whole right heel. Apply a positive charge to the left set of toes (including big toe) and the negative charge to the whole left heel.

Korton explained that the details of the process will vary between individuals - do what feels comfortable to you. Thy self be the director of the healing and thou that is God/Goddess sends forth the vibration to be used.

CHAPTER 1, CHRIST JESUS, 1994 UPDATE ON "YOUR PHYSICAL IMMORTALITY"

Your own physical immortality and Ascension opportunity are now possible when you commit yourself to an inner self-cleansing and healing, to total commitment to God, and to the expression of non-judgmental love to self and others. We offer you this "Garment of Light Meditation for Ascension" so you might become an Ascended Master in your own right during this lifetime! We have released this special initiation meditation to several excellent teachers and many more will be bringing its presentation to those light workers determined to claim their inter-dimensional identity.

The purpose of the "Garment of Light Meditation" practice, then, is to teach you how to acquire a 55-foot crystalline energy disk of light around your body that can be accelerated to the speed of light. When you understand God energy well enough to do this one experience you may then translate or transform your physical body into other dimensions. YOU WILL NEVER AGAIN DIE.

The White Brotherhood's Order of Melchizedek and the Office of the Christ are working on this amazing event together since both have heavenly teachers involved on your behalf from our dimensions, and because most light workers are spiritually related to one or both of these teacher groups. This means there are greater numbers focused on the specific purpose of getting you ascended as quickly and safely as possible!–if that is your true desire.

This form of transformation we bring you has many advantages over the kind of crucified body death I used in order to resurrect, and you need not go through the old pattern I selected. No one here wishes your crucifixion unless you choose it to prove a point and leave your own model for others to remember.

When you attain your "Garment of Light" body, you can return to the higher dimensions, visit other cosmic locations and continue to grow in awareness, consciousness and service to God. Yes, when you enter that holy coordinate point where the energies of the Mother/Father fuel your DNA shift from cocoon to butterfly, from earthen to galactic identity, you will truly be home.

There will be many teachers of Immortality, but unless they give you an initiation using love of God, self, and brother as a precursor to the meditation we bring, and know the meditation themselves, your transformation will be arduous if not impossible. I therefore urge you to use your spiritual discretion in selecting your meditation teacher.

As God's heavenly realms and galactic rhythms and cycles expand all of life into higher and higher dimensions, and a deeper relationship to the Source of ALL, you may hasten your own personal Ascension, if you wish it. But let me assure you that even if you do not learn the meditation and use it for inter-dimensional translation, you are a part of heaven and to heaven you will return! Have no fear, beloveds, rather rejoice that so many will be with us very soon and that the Divine plan on earth is being fulfilled. That seal was placed in your genetic structure long ago and your DNA is now being upgraded even as we speak. We are doing our part to awaken you and assist in the glorious expansion of life everywhere. Your dear Mother Earth and those who reside upon her need more loving helpers in our dimensions to assist in humanity's rebirth just as we need loving beings alive on the planet.

You are needed, beloveds, one place or the other. Both are necessary and valuable services! Whether you choose to ascend and volunteer your energy inter-dimensionally, or remain on earth, you are loved! Never doubt it.

Eternally your teacher and elder brother,

Christ Jesus

(Note from Virginia: If you will send a stamped, self-addressed envelope to the Share Foundation's office, we will provide a list of those meditation teachers of Immortality we have been asked to share.)

COSMIC REVELATION
Ann Valentin & Virginia Essene

The authors channel inspirational wisdom for the 21st century in this book of cosmic guidance and spiritual illumination. 181 pp.

ISBN 0-937147-02-8   Paper, $9.95

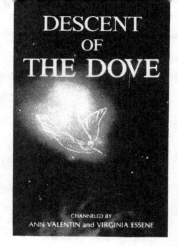

DESCENT OF THE DOVE
Ann Valentin & Virginia Essene

Explains how the spiritual realms have speeded up humanity's perception of time by 20% and suggests ways to successfully stretch the remaining 80% through knowledge of the "Cosmic Compass" and more. 206 pp.

ISBN 0-937147-03-6   Paper, $9.95

NEW TEACHINGS
For an Awakening Humanity
Virginia Essene

Learn more about the true reason for Jesus' mission 2000 years ago and share a glimpse of the wondrous future that awaits us on earth. Highly recommended by Judith Skutch, Eileen Caddy and John Price. Spanish edition also. 208 pp.

ISBN 0-937147-00-1   Paper, $8.95

SECRET TRUTHS
A Young Adult's Guide for Creating Peace
Virginia Essene

In this book for all ages, the author recognizes people in their teens and twenties as souls of high spiritual level whose memories have been sealed, and whose trials reflect all of humanity's struggle to awaken. 142 pp.

ISBN 0-937147-05-2   Paper, $8.95

Don't Miss the Love Corps Newsletter!

Spiritual Education Endeavors Publishing Co.
1556 Halford Avenue, #288
Santa Clara, CA 95051, U.S.A.
(408) 245-5457

The Blue Rose Connection
presents
Orpheus Phylos & The Archangel Michael

Orpheus Phylos is a renowned metaphysician and channel for her mentor, the Archangel Michael. Orpheus brings a wide and varied background to her work as counselor, teacher and lecturer. Her study of metaphysics and New Age philosophy began more than twenty years ago, progressing through basic metaphysical tools that led to a greater perception and understanding which culminated in telepathy and channeling. Orpheus has a Ph.D. in Hypnosis/Hypnotherapy and a Minister of Divinity Degree.

Speaking and working through Orpheus, the Archangel Michael brings to Earth the transmutable blue flame to stamp out negativity by transmuting it into the four L's...Law, Life, Light and Love. Michael uses the technique of humor, leading to acceptance, to accomplish a higher vbibratory level, thereby assisting those who are ready to attain self-mastery and achieve alignment with the higher forces of guidance. Being the overseer of the fire element, Michael has come to uplift the frequencies of Planet Earth for the harmonic evolvement into the Golden Age Dawn.

Orpheus and Michael form a unique partnership to provide spiritual counseling, teach seminars and classes, and to lecture to groups both small and large. New Age wisdom is presented with gentle warmth, penetrating insight and much humor. Orpheus and Michael are dedicated to teaching each one to hear his or her own guidance, thereby connecting with their own inner voice.

In 1992, The Archangel Michael and Orpheus established the Carrousel Mountain Retreat, which is based on Michael's philosophies. Functions include the Initiations on the levels of Neophytes, Adepts and the Illuminaries.

For videos, audio tapes, books and further information of the Carrousel Mountain Retreat, phone or write :

Orpheus Phylos
Carrousel Mountain Retreat
P.O. Box 1193, Bandon, OR 97411.
Phone (503) 347-6100.

CAROLE AUSTEN M.A., A.T.R. (Art Therapist
Registered), specialist in educational, personal and
professional career consulting through accessing
higher intelligence. Carole entertained audiences on
the Arsenio Hall Show and on L.A. Good Morning,
and hosted her own "ASK THE SOURCE" live radio
show. Carole brings in specific and helpful advice
directly from celestial beings and your cosmic guides
(*the SOURCE*) who draw portraits of themselves
through her. She taught at the University of
Humanistic Studies and at UCSD Extension, and is a
teaching minister of the Paul Soloman Foundation.
For *SOURCE* transmissions call 408-625-6513.

HILARION

Channeled by John C. Fox

As an electronics engineer (Northwestern University, 1974) Jon's interest in new energy devices led him to channeling as a source of new knowledge and principles. The energy expressing itself through Jon calls itself "**Hilarion**" and is available to assist the evolution of humans on the Earth **now**. This energy is especially concerned with humanity's capacity for Universal Love, and speaks often of heart-opening and what each person must do to take our place as the beacons of love and light we truly are. As well, **Hilarion** provides enlightening and revolutionary technical information for astrologers, scientists, physicists, artists and healers. This guidance has helped many people in understanding personal issues, past lives, life purpose, vibrational healing and the symbolism of the body.

Among **Hilarion**'s works channeled through Jon are the books by Gurudas: <u>Gem Elixers and Vibrational Healing</u>, Vol. I and II, <u>The Spiritual Properties of Herbs</u> and <u>Flower Essences, the Revised Edition</u>. Hilarion, through Jon, has been a guest on radio and television talk shows. A videotape and audio tapes of group channelings on subjects of wide interest are available. Jon has been building devices and doing experiments channeled by **Hilarion**, principally in New Physics and in areas of healing. A most recent project with Pegasus Products, Inc. in Boulder, CO, is the creation of Starlight Elixers - a distillation of individual star energy captured within liquid form. They are a continuation of the potent energies the stars have long been gifting to the peoples of the Earth.

Personal as well as research readings with **Hilarion** are available through Jon in Nevada City, California. Telephone consultations, "remote readings" and group channelings, as well as public group events, are scheduled in the northern California area. For a catalogue of **Hilarion** publications, or for information on scheduling an appointment with Jon and **Hilarion**, write to:

Jon C. Fox
P.O. Box 2209
Nevada City, CA 95959

GROWING CURRENTS OF LOVE

"Awakening to a New Reality"

For more
information,
write:

**Nova 8/Norman
Communities of Light
P.O. Box 11919
Pueblo, CO 81001 USA**

PORTALS OF LIGHT

presents
Publications and tapes of material
channeled through Tuieta.

Conclave Series

The ongoing record of meetings dealing with the effects of the infusion of energies designed to awaken the Christ Consciousness sleeping within each of us. These meetings, held aboard the command ships, progressively deal with changes in governmental, financial, religious and educational systems; new communication devices; earth and weather changes; grey men; walk-ins; changing relationships; children; evacuation plans; handling fear; potential food shortages, ETs, and more.

Talks with The Masters Series

Each Master shares a series of teachings to assist the reader to grow in their own spiritual understanding and knowing. Topics include: Loving thyself; the Christos within; honor; faith; peace; will; judgment; discernment; service and servitude; the dark brotherhood; the bio-organism; fear; pain; integration, and more.

Letters from Home Series

Given by ones of the Ashtar Command, these 'letters' address: Observations of our present state; possible intervention; preparation for today, tomorrow and the New Day; reunion with our brothers/sisters of other realms; eagles; sighting of ships; life on the ships; nuclear war; planetary unrest and more.

The Elemental Kingdom

Tobias and others discuss their life and purpose in working with us, Mother Earth, the Nature Kingdom, the Angelic Kingdom and more.

For more information about this material, newsletter, other books/manuscripts and tapes, write:

Portals of Light, Inc.
P.O. Box 15621
Fort Wayne, IN 46885

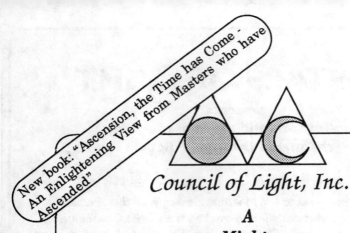

THE PLEIADIANS

CHANNELED BY BARBARA J. MARCINIAK

The Pleiadians are a collective of extraterrestrials from the star system the Pleiades. They have been speaking through the body of the vehicle, Barbara J. Marciniak since May 18, 1988. They say they were conceived on the Harmonic Convergence, and birthed in Athens, Greece nine months later.

The Pleiadian collective was originally composed of seventy-five to one hundred entities, now they often refer to themselves as Pleiadian Plus, indicating a joining of forces with other extraterrestrials. They are here to assist us in our awakening in remembering who we are.

Barbara J. Marciniak travels throughout the United States and the world with the Pleiadians. She facilitates tours to power sites such as Peru, Egypt, Mexico, Bali & Greece. When not traveling Barbara resides in Raleigh, North Carolina where she conducts class sessions and transformational workshops. Her first book: *"The Bringers of the Dawn: The New Evolution of Man"* will be published in 1992.

MARK NICLAS

Mark is the facilitator/founder of the Dove Center and is a channel for Spiritual and Galactic teachers of Light. He conducts "Circles of Light" around the world, in which channeled information or lectures are given to assist in the re-awakening of Spiritual remembrance for Mother Earth and her children.

The Dove Center has a bi-monthly newsletter called:

FLIGHT OF THE DOVE.

Other books by Mark include the three-volume series titled:

<u>CALLING ALL WORKERS OF THE LIGHT</u>

Please contact Mark at his new address:

Mark Niclas
1415 Victoria Street
#615
Honolulu, HI 96822

(808) 524-8340

PARTICIPATION QUESTIONNAIRE
AND ORDER FORM

TO: S.E.E. Publishing Company
c/o The SHARE FOUNDATION*
1556 Halford Avenue, #288
Santa Clara, CA 95051 USA

Please send information on how I can help disseminate
<u>New Cells, New Bodies, NEW LIFE!</u> to:
❏ Friends, Bookstores, Churches, other Organizations
❏ Other Countries

I wish to donate my skills and/or time for:
❏ Secretarial/Clerical ❏ Fund-raising ❏ Graphic Arts
❏ Word Processing ❏ Bookkeeping & Accounting
❏ Public Speaking ❏ Translating ❏ Publicity
❏ Promotion/Publication
❏ Other
  (specify):_____

I have the following equipment and technical know-how for:
❏ Personal Computer: Make/Model _____
❏ CB Radio ❏ Ham Radio Equipment

Here's my I.R.S. approved donation for the **LOVE CORPS**
efforts. ❏ $1,000 or more ❏ $500 ❏ $250
         ❏ $100 ❏ Other $_____

I would like to help publicize <u>New Cells, New Bodies,</u>
<u>NEW LIFE!</u> ❏ On TV ❏ In newspapers, magazines
❏ On Radio ❏ Other (specify): _____

❏   I would like to be a networker or contact person for the
    LOVE CORPS in my area.
        Check if holding a meditation group others may
        attend._____
        May we give others your address and telephone
        number? _____

*The Share Foundation (non-profit I.R.S. Fed. EIN 94-2699567)

(Continued on reverse)

Please send me copies of the following **books:**   (U.S. $)

New Cells, New Bodies, NEW LIFE! @ $11.95 $_____

Descent of the Dove . . . . @ $9.95 $_____

**Secret Truths: A Young Adult's
Guide for Creating Peace** . . . .@ $8.95 $_____

New Teachings for an Awakening Humanity:
    English ed. . . . .@ $8.95 $_____
    Spanish ed. **Nuevas Ensenanzas** . . .@ $9.95 $_____

Minus Love Corps discount if applicable** . . . . $(_____)
                                          Subtotal . . . . $_____
Plus 8.25% sales tax (California residents only) . . . . $_____
Plus shipping & handling for one book:***
    (Surface rates: $2 for U.S.A.; $3 for foreign) . . . . $_____
Plus shipping for each additional book:***
    ($1 for U.S.A.; $1.25 for foreign). . . . . $_____

Love Corps donation (tax deductible). . . . . $_____

Please send me the **Love Corps Newsletter**:
☐ 1993 issues available upon request @ $4/issue.
    Please specify: J/F, M/A, M/J, J/A, S/O, N/D $_____
☐ One year (bi-monthly) 1994 subscription = $24 $_____
☐ Canadian & other international = $30 (airmail) $_____
                              TOTAL ENCLOSED $_____

Please PRINT (this information is for your mailing label)

_____
Name

_____
Address

_____
City   State/Province   Zip Code

(_____)_____
Area Code   Telephone Number (optional)

** Love Corps discounts:
        5 to 9 books - take off 10%
        10 or more books - take off 20%
*** Please request shipping rates for first class or air mail.

LOVE CORPS NETWORKING

The term **Love Corps** was coined in the book <u>New Teachings for an Awakening Humanity</u>. It is a universal alliance of all human beings of good will who seek both inner personal peace and its planetary application. Thus the worldwide Love Corps family is committed to achieving inner peace through meditation and self-healing and to sharing that peace in groups where the unity of cooperation can be applied toward the preservation of all life.

Virginia Essene frequently travels around the United States and the world to link Love Corps energies, to share additional information not included in **New Cells, New Bodies, NEW LIFE; New Teachings; Secret Truths; Cosmic Revelation** and **Descent of the Dove** books, and to encourage humanity's achievement of peace and the preservation of all life upon planet earth.

If you would like to be involved in the Love Corps endeavors, to participate with us in seminars, or to have an individual counseling session, please write for information so we can possibly include your area in our itinerary.

This Time of Awakening brings a new spiral of information, to move each of us to a higher level of inner peace and planetary involvement. You are encouraged to accept the responsibility of this evolutionary opportunity and immediately unite efforts with other people in creating peaceful attitudes and conditions on our planet.

SHARE Foundation
1556 Halford Ave., #288
Santa Clara, CA 95051
USA

NOTES